The World of
Indian Civilization

The World of Indian Civilization

Text by **Gustave Le Bon**

Translated by David Macrae

Tudor Publishing Company

New York

Table of Contents

*Frontispiece: one of the giant statues
in the underground temple at Elephanta.*

Credits : Archives : 5, 6, 22, 27, 30a, 40, 47, 86 - Bourdelon-Weiss-Viollet : 59a - Christophe : 121 - Giraudon : 13, 14, 20, 29, 30b, 32, 33, 35, 36, 37, 38, 44, 48, 51, 54, 55, 57, 58, 60, 68, 74, 87, 90, 93a, 94 113, 138, 140, 141, 143 - Lauros-Giraudon : 17, 53, 78, 91 - Mahatta-Wiss-Viollet : 10 - Roger-Viollet : 2, 18, 24, 25a, 25b, 50, 59b, 66, 67b, 71, 72, 75, 76, 77a, 77b, 80, 81, 82, 83a, 83b, 83c, 84, 85, 88, 89, 92, 101b, 104, 105, 106, 107, 109, 110, 111, 112, 114, 115, 116, 118, 119a, 119b, 124, 125, 126, 127, 128, 129, 130, 131, 132, 133, 134, 137a, 137b, 137c, 142, 144 - San-Viollet : 63, 64, 93b, 102, 122, 135 - Weiss-Viollet : 26, 101a.

© *Editions Minerva, S.A., Genève, 1974*
ISBN 0-8148-0581-7
Printer, Industria Gráfica, S.A.
Tuset, 19 Barcelona · San Vicente dels Horts 1974
Depósito legal B. 16043-1974
Printed in Spain

Library of Congress Cataloging in Publication Data

Le Bon, Gustave, 1841-1931
The World of Indian Civilization

(World of ancient civilizations, no. 11)
1. India-Civilization. I. Title
DS 421.1443 1974   915.4'03   74-1208

*Statuette, about
2,000 B.C. (National
Museum, Delhi).*

1. The Vedas and Their Times

The documents from which we can reconstruct the civilization of India over a period of nearly 4,000 years, when it was inhabited by people at vastly different cultural levels, far outnumber those from which we can retrace its history. Sacred writings such as the Vedas, great epic poems such as the Ramayana and the Mahabharata and ancient codes such as the laws of Manu enable us to form a reasonably clear idea of social conditions at the time these works were produced. The hundreds of fables, myths and legends left by ancient India paint a vivid picture of the feelings, thoughts and opinions of the people who created them, while the historical remains and unfortunately all too rare eye-witness accounts, such as those of Megasthenes the Greek ambassador and of the Chinese pilgrims Fa-Hian and Hiouen-Thsang, form a valuable supplement to our other sources of information.

The Aryan civilization made its appearance in the north-west of India about 15,000 B.C. It has left us no stone remains, and there is nothing to indicate that it ever built in stone. Its sole legacy to the world is the vast religious compendium known as the Vedas, consisting of works written at very different times. The most important is the *Rig Veda*, which must have been composed no later than 1,000 B.C. Properly interpreted, it recreates for us the

5

language, religious beliefs and the ways of life and thought of the people who wrote it. It was not until the 19th century that these ancient writings first became known in Europe.

The name of Aryan has been given to a white-skinned black-haired people speaking a lost tongue known as Aryan, which was the forerunner of Sanskrit and which, more than fifteen centuries before the Christian era, was brought through the Kabul passes in the north-west of India. The people who spoke it were semi-nomad semi-sedentary tribes, skilled in agriculture, endowed, like so many nomads, with a vivid imagination, and resembling in their way of life the ancient Persians as described by Herodotus.

They advanced slowly from the Indus to the Ganges and from there to the Brahmaputra, conquering as they went the dark-skinned straight-haired peoples and the Turanians who had occupied the land before them. From being nomadic they gradually settled down.

The origins of these invaders, who played such an important part in the history of India, are wrapped in mystery.

It is generally acknowledged that before the 2nd century B.C. the first Aryans were living in what is now Turkestan on the upper reaches of the Oxus. They are then thought to have split up into two major migratory groups, one moving towards Europe and the other towards Iran. After living for a long time in Persia, Bactria and Sogdiana, the descendants of those emigrants must have continued southwards and, after crossing the Hindu

Assorted seals, from the Indus (about 2,000 B.C.).

Kush, entered India. If this theory is accepted, Europeans and Hindus have descended from the selfsame Asiatic tribes.

It is merely a hypothesis, though, based solely on the fact that our European languages, such as Latin, Greek and German, have a common parentage with old Persian and Sanskrit in the similarity of their roots. Hindus and Europeans are undoubtedly connected linguistically, but we now know that we cannot always conclude from similarities of language that there is kinship of race as well.

In Vedic times, the family and the race were the twin pillars of society. They were not separated by any tribal group, clan or government. Above the family there was only the race, while below there was nothing at all, since the individual had no separate existence but was part of his ancestors and descendants.

Religion itself was simply the worship of race and family. The gods were looked upon as being one with the forefathers of the race. Marriage and procreation were sacred acts. The transmission of life from father to son through the mother was the mysterious passage of Agni, the divine fire and principle of fertility, the lord and creator of the universe, through the woman's body to perpetuate eternal life.

To form an alliance with a foreigner or to die without leaving a son were the greatest of misfortunes for the Aryans. To corrupt the race was to lose for ever the divine bond

7

by which every Aryan was united to Agni.

To die without male issue had equally terrible consequences. The son assured his ancestors of immortality by his veneration and the sacrifices he offered up to them. Should any interruption occur in these, the shades of his forefathers would be condemned to limbo, and the family would cease to exist forever.

Monogamy seems to have been customary among the Vedic Aryans. However, to judge from later practices, princes and rich men probably had several wives. The main reason for the introduction of polygamy among the Aryans was the imperative need to have male heirs. A man whose first wife bore him nothing but daughters was therefore constrained to take a second wife.

A young girl was allowed to choose her husband, and even if several claimants fought for the honor of her hand in a mock battle, as occasionally happened, they could not engage in combat without her permission, and if she refused to crown the victor, the matter went no further. The Vedas describe the flowering of love and the first relations between young men and girls in the most delicate terms. As there was no happiness for the Aryans, in this world or the next, outside the family, they were drawn, in their own interests and in that of religion—in other words by the most powerful motives that can move the human heart—to attach the greatest possible importance to marriage.

The ceremonies associated with a marriage bore the stamp of that religious fervor which marked every event in family life. They were made impressive by the solemnity of the prayers and sacrifices and of the vows uttered, and joyful by the splendor of the apparel worn, the number of people present and the rejoicings to which everyone gave themselves up.

At the beginning of the Vedic period, before the Aryans reached the Ganges basin and were occupying the vast plains of the country of seven rivers, watered by the Indus and its tributaries, there were no traces of political institutions, of castes or of government to be found among them.

The basis of their society was the family, and society itself was composed of the whole race irrespective of functions or classes. Each head of a family made the sacrifices, farmed the land and went to war. These occupations which, when separated, formed the basis of the caste system, were then inextricably intertwined.

There was no tie between one village and another, nor was there any supreme power over the chieftains. The hazards of war brought them together, sometimes in large numbers, under a single command, but the concept of kingship did not gain ground until later. We shall find it among the Aryans when they settled in the Ganges basin, but in Vedic times the king was merely the equivalent of a war lord. A king with ministers, who levied taxes regularly and governed the whole race, was unknown during the Vedic period.

Bronze statuette from the Indus:
a dancing girl.

Kingship was in any case a purely nominal concept in India. In Aryan times the basic political unit was like a village, but more rigidly structured and forming a small but well-organized republic, with a chieftain in the fortress exercising wide authority under the title of rajah; this is the political system which has always prevailed in India and which the conquerors, whoever they were, were forced to respect, because it was unshakable.

Thus, many centuries ago in a still unformed society, we see the first traces of the basic system of organization which was to subsist for countless years.

We also find the first traces of the caste system which, from being loosely-defined and fluid when the classes were anxious only to distinguish between themselves, subsequently became so inflexible when it came under the influence of ethnic concepts that it ended by creating an unbridgeable gap between the races.

We can follow, from the Vedas, the widening of the gap between priests and warriors which was narrow to begin with but then increased steadily. The division of functions did not end there. While the sacrificer devoted himself more and more to the performance of the sacred rites and the composition of religious chants, and the warrior spent his time in daring forays or tests of prowess, what would have happened to the land, what would it have yielded, if others had not devoted themselves untiringly to cultivating it? A third caste thus emerged—that of the farmers.

In one of the last poems of the Rig Veda,

the three castes appear as distinct entities and have already been given the names of Brahman, Kshatriya and Vaishya.

The fourth caste, that of Shudras, was formed later from the conquered hordes after they had been assimilated into the Aryan civilization.

The most important division, which was undoubtedly the first to occur, was the separation between priests and warriors. The Brahmans, who occupied a position midway between men and the gods, became more and more exacting; they came to regard themselves as wholly superior beings and successfully imposed this image of themselves on the rest of the people.

The inheritance of functions, which marks the definitive establishment of the caste system, does not seem to have been an inviolable rule among the Vedic Aryans, but it had already begun to be customary among them. In some families, the sacred chants were transmitted from father to son together with the duties of the sacrificer. It is thanks to this custom, in fact, that the Vedas have been so marvellously preserved to this day.

From reading the Vedas, we can easily picture the everyday life of the Aryans in all its details.

Their fabrics were made of wool or linen, sometimes interwoven with gold thread. Spinning was done by the women, and the workers wove with the aid of a shuttle. They wore shoes which they tied around the ankle, as we can see from the verse which speaks of Indra the god who was always active and moving from place to place: "whose shoes were never untied".

Their chariots were ornamented with bright metal plaques. They were built on rimmed wheels and axles.

The horses were attached to the chariots and driven by reins, bit and whip.

The warriors were dressed in brightly-polished armor.

Together with war and its related occupations, agriculture was the main activity of the Aryans.

Living in the Indus basin, which was often ravaged by drought, they learnt to follow the course of the seasons and to scan the sky for signs of health-giving rain.

The Aryans tilled the soil with plows pulled by oxen. They gathered in the harvest on carts also pulled by oxen.

The Aryans' herds were one of their main sources of wealth. The cow, which provided milk—their major food—was held in great honor. It was cared for and venerated; in fact, it was virtually an object of worship.

Milk and butter were the staple foods of the Aryans, and were offered as libations to the gods. Melted butter was poured on firewood to add to the force and brilliance of Agni—the fire. Honey is praised throughout the Vedas. Other favorite foods which were offered to the gods were meal cakes and barley fritters.

The Aryans also ate flesh. They were great hunters, killing game with bows and arrows or trapping it. Their fishing was done with nets.

One of the causes of the sudden and profound afflictions and reversals of fortunes suffered by the Aryans was their uncontrolla-ble passion for gambling. Games of chance, and dicing in particular, absorbed them to such a point that they sometimes lost in a single game their riches, their houses, their fields, their children, their wives and even their own liberty. The misery caused by this fatal passion of theirs in described in the Vedas in the most somber terms.

The Aryans usually buried their dead, and there are many passages in the Vedas which speak of the funeral ceremonies. Here, expressed in poetic form, is the farewell addressed by a living person to the dead:

"Go", says he to the dead, "go seek the Earth, that great and good mother, who, ever youthful, stretches beyond our horizons, that she may be as a soft carpet for him who has honored the gods by his gifts.

"O Earth, awake. Let him suffer no longer. Be gentle and watchful over him. O Earth, cover him as a mother covers her child with a fold of her garment.

"May the Earth rise up for thee. I dig this tomb so that thy bones may rest in peace. May thy ancestors watch over this tomb. May Yama make it his habitation.

"The days are for me as the arrows for the feathers they bear."

The religious beliefs of the Aryans were rather nebulous. There was no clearly-defined deity for them.

Their religious chants embody a variety of concepts. Everything is to be found there, from the worship of the forces of nature to pantheism, polytheism and monotheism.

Nothing is more difficult than to try to classify or arrange the Aryan gods in any sort of hierarchy.

Among the ill-defined gods and symbols with their inextricable confusion of powers and status which abound in Vedic mythology, those who are most often mentioned are:

Agni, the personification of fire, and Soma, the fermented liquid which adds force to Agni. Agni engendered the gods, the world and universal life. Soma makes the gods immortal and fills men with vigor. Soma also engendered the earth and the sky, Indra and Vishnu. Together with Agni he forms the sky and the stars.

One of the most important gods for the Aryans was Indra, lord of the sky. He is a war-like god, who is depicted standing upright on his war chariot—the veritable apotheosis of an Aryan tribal chief.

The great epic poems of the Mahabharata and of the Ramayana, although considerably later than the first Vedic chants, are still genuinely Aryan works.

After reading them, it is easy to see how far our ideas of godhead differ from those of the Aryans. The power of the gods is often praised in those poems, but when the gods are drawn into combat with men of spirits, even the most powerful do not always emerge the victors.

We learn from the Vedas that the gods they believed in resembled those beings of ambiguous aspect which the ancient naturalists classed sometimes as animals and sometimes

as plants. In trying to classify them, the following points stand out from the over-all body of beliefs set forth in the Vedas:

1. Worship of the forces of nature;
2. Personification of those forces as divine beings;
3. Belief in the immortality of the soul;
4. Ancestor worship;
5. The belief that nature, men and the gods are under the sway of another and all-powerful god, usually Indra;
6. The constant tendency to express religious beliefs in material ways with the result that religion degenerated into a self-interested exchange of gifts between the gods and men, the latter offering up their animals and the fruits of the earth as sacrifices and the former bestowing an abundance of rain when needed, health and wealth.

The beliefs with regard to a future life are equally nebulous and variable in the Vedas. It was thought that the individual returned to the elements after his death and that his soul acquired a new body, a concept which seems to herald the future belief in metempsychosis. The belief in the soul as the immortal principle inhabiting the body but superior to it and constituting the essential human personality was also to be seen in the Vedas.

The belief in the immortality of the soul gave rise to the reverence felt for *Pitris* or ancestors. According to the Aryans, their dead ancestors could not be happy in their

future life unless their family was perpetuated on earth and offered up regular prayers and sacrifices to them.

The idea of a supreme God, creator of all mortal and immortal beings, and holding sway over the immense mass of men, ancestors and gods is also to be found in a rather rudimentary sense in the Vedas. Each god celebrated in song seems for the writer to be the most important of all or even the only god. It can also happen that the gods are regarded as one and the same divine being under different names.

The Aryans' code of ethics was primitive but strict. Charity, kindness to animals and faithfulness in friendship are virtually the only obligations given prominence in the Vedas.

Chakra, weapon of Vishnu.

2. The Brahmanic Period

The seat of the Aryan civilization was the basin of the Indus, but it was in the Ganges basin that the Brahman civilization reached its apogee.

Nearly a thousand years elapsed between the heyday of the two civilizations, and during that time the conquerors of India moved steadily eastwards. By then they were the masters of the whole of Hindustan proper, stretching from the sea of Oman to the gulf of Bengal and from the Himalayas to the Vindhya mountains. The former inhabitants of that vast and rich area were utterly subjugated; they ceased to resist, accepted the alien yoke and intermingled with their conquerors.

The Brahman civilization was at its height in the 3rd and 4th centuries B.C. It was undoubtedly at that time that the laws of Manu, the *Manava-Dharma-Sastra*, later to become India's civil and political code, were compiled.

This compendium was originally thought to be older. W. Jones, the English expert, placed it in the 7th century B.C. and other writers in the 5th century B.C., but a more recent opinion, which seems to be better-founded, places it no further back than the 2nd or 3rd century B.C.

The *Manava-Dharma-Sastra* is our most reliable source of information on the Brahma-

Left: a relief cut in rock, commemorating the descent of the Ganges (6th c.).
Right: goddess of the river.

15

nic period. It is the equivalent of the *Rig Veda* for the Vedic period.

We have indicated how functions were separated and tended to become hereditary towards the end of the Vedic period. This is thought to have been one of the main reasons for the development of the caste system, but it does not suffice in itself to explain it.

The Vedic Aryans were already concerned with the need to maintain the purity of the race, to show a scrupulous respect for genealogy and to preserve the old families. These also became the main concerns of their legislators once the final subjugation of northern India scattered the relatively small band of conquerors among the vast hordes of the vanquished.

This is what the law of Manu has to say in this respect:

"Any part of the country where men of mixed race are born to sully the purity of the castes shall be forthwith destroyed together with its inhabitants.

"However distinguished a man's family may be, if he is born of mixed caste he shall inherit in some degree the innate sinfulness of his parents.

"The want of noble sentiments, roughness of speech, cruelty and indifference to duty are the marks here on earth of the man who owes his being to a woman worthy of disdain."

The castes as specified by Manu were four in number: the priests; the Kshatriyas or warriors; the farmers, moneylenders and

Ancient divinity (Benares).

16

merchants; and, lowest of all, the Shudras, who did not even have a specific occupation and whose sole function was to serve the others.

A man had to marry within his own caste or conceivably into a slightly lower caste but whoever married a Shudras was dishonored, lost his caste, became an object of universal scorn in this world and was doomed to suffer in the next. Shudras could marry only among themselves.

The Brahmans as a caste were infinitely superior to all other people. Because of their power and rights and the respect in which they were held, they were looked upon as demigods rather than mere mortals. Their exceptionally privileged position was due to their purity of blood, to their supposed power to intercede with the gods through prayer, and to the authority of the learning they spent their lives in acquiring.

The privileges they enjoyed were of course counterbalanced by duties. Their life was divided into four parts: childhood, dedicated to studying the sacred writings and religious rites under special teachers; youth, when they married and became fathers and heads of families because, as the Brahman's functions were hereditary, his first duty was to have a son; middle age, which was spent in retirement from the world, celibacy and austerity; and old age, when the Brahman, having become sufficiently pure to communicate directly with the gods, gave himself up to meditation and preparing for death.

Brahmans who were poor were allowed to

A road, between Ellora and Aurengabad.

19

*Above: engraved stone used as an administrative document.
Below: coin in the form of a bar.*

perform certain duties and even to engage in commerce. In general, however, they depended on the charity of the Kshatriyas or warriors. To give to a Brahman was the most meritorious act a Hindu could perform.

Megasthenes was a witness to the honors paid to the Brahmins and admired their philosophy which he thought resembled that of Socrates and Pythagoras.

The Kshatriyas or warriors devoted themselves to military duties and had no other activity or occupation. In times of peace, they necessarily led an idle life. They had to be always ready to fight and to respond to the first call, and their main duty was to protect the people. Knowing that the Kshatriyas were guarding the frontiers, the Vaishyas could farm the land without fear.

The Kshatriyas and the Brahmans were the twin pillars of society, but the former were thought of as greatly inferior to the latter. This is what the law of Manu has to say on the subject:

"The Kshatriyas cannot prosper without the Brahmans; the Brahmans cannot survive without the Kshatriyas, but through the union of the priestly caste with the military caste, both can advance in this world and the next.

"A Brahman of ten years old and a Kshatriya of 100 years old should be regarded as father and son, and of the two the Brahman, is the father and should be respected as such."

This passage reveals how great a distance lay between the first two castes, but it was nothing in comparison with the abyss that

Sarcophagus from an ancient tomb.

yawned between them and the rest of the people. The Kshatriyas were in some respects on a par with the Brahmins, and the words quoted indicate the close alliance between the two castes. The Vaisyas were far below them, while the Shudras were not recognized as members of society at all.

The Vaishya caste consisted of the farmers, the merchants and the moneylenders. They were people in their second reincarnation, but they had been initiated later than the Kshatriyas, who in their turn had been admitted later than the Brahmans.

However modest the occupation of a Vaishya, he never lowered himself to the point of becoming a servant. He had his house, and his family of which he was the respected head. For a Brahman Hindu, there was nothing more humiliating than to enter the service of another. To obey orders unquestioningly was the lot of the beasts of burden and of the Shudras.

Some drops of Aryan blood undoubtedly still ran in the veins of the Vaishyas, but it was very mixed. As for the Shudras, they were the native inhabitants, the vile beings with whom an alliance meant the loss of honor forever—the dregs of creation who were more despised than any brute beast. From the Brahman standpoint that was understandable, because neither the dog nor the horse represented any threat for the future of the Aryan race, whereas the Aryans lived in perpetual fear of being swallowed up forever by the multitude of black-skinned Shudras they had vanquished. No sooner would they cease to keep these conquered peoples at a distance than their peaceful infiltration would immediately threaten to obliterate the last traces of that ancient race that was the pride of the Brahmans.

During the Brahmanic period, the Hindus built entire cities, which rose in splendor on the banks of the Ganges. These glorious cities were a far cry from the humble villages of the Vedic Aryans.

The buildings of that time have left few traces, but the best-preserved remains, such as the bas-reliefs of Bharhut and the pillars of Ashoka, demonstrate that the Hindus had become highly-skilled in architecture.

It seems probable that the early buildings in India were made of wood and brick, and that the stone buildings were merely copies of them. This probability is borne out by the descriptions given by Megasthenes and by the investigations made in Nepal.

In any case, there is no doubt that the Hindus possessed large cities at the time of Megasthenes. He describes the great city of Pataliputra in terms which give a clear idea of its magnitude, its power and its splendor.

It lay on the banks of the Ganges in a long parallelogram. It was protected by a wall which encircled it and was in its turn surround-

ed by a broad ditch. The King's palace, the bazaars, the shops full of valuable merchandise, the splendid processions which wound through the streets, all these aroused the admiration of Megasthenes.

During the Brahmanic period, the King's power was absolute. He had to be obeyed like a god and, no sooner had he been crowned, even though he might have come to the throne by a crime, he was regarded as the incarnation of the divine will and power.

The law of Manu says that one must not show contempt towards a monarch even in childhood by saying of him that he is simply a human being, because he is in reality a great god who has chosen to assume human form.

Their rule seems to have been benevolent enough and did not weigh too heavily on their subjects. The Brahmans occupied what was virtually a higher position because of the prestige of their caste. The king had to follow their counsels and to make gifts to them, and they themselves through their prayers had the power to make his reign prosperous and glorious or to bring down on his head the anger and curses of the gods. The king came from the Kshatriya caste. The Kshatriyas were his companions in arms and respected him as a soldier respects his leader.

Bust of a woman, or mother-goddess, about 300 B.C. (Archeological Museum, Mathura).

The king's power was therefore at its most absolute over the Vaisha caste. All the men in that caste were his farmers. It was for him that they cultivated the land and engaged in trade. For him, or rather for the State, because, although all tax revenue went directly to the King, he had to draw on his own funds to maintain the army and to carry out public works.

Inspectors who went throughout the provinces and the towns and into the smallest villages kept a check on agricultural production and on the value and sales price of the goods marketed in order to determine and collect the king's share of each transaction.

Although the king held absolute power, he could not abuse his privileges. Confined to the palace, and constrained to lead a regular life and to perform the numerous duties expected of him as specified in the laws of Manu, his main concern seems to have been to escape the dagger and poison. Perilous and difficult though it was, his position was envied. The fortunate assassin who stepped into his shoes was regarded as a divine being as soon as he held the throne and sceptre, and as his only fear until then had been to fail, it was only by strict and constant precautions that the life of the sovereign could be protected. These precautions are recommended by the laws of Manu themselves. The king should have around him only people of weak and timid nature who would be too fearful to plot against him; he should change the position of his bed as often as possible, and he should

Elephants on a frieze at Konarak (above) and at Ellora (lower right). Opposite: Lifesize monolithic elephant, at Konarak.

never become inebriated because he might in that state be killed by one of his wives who could then with impunity marry his successor.

No one was entitled to live in the palace apart from the king and his wives; even the guard was lodged outside it.

From time to time, a splendid procession of richly caparisoned elephants, armed women, archers and guards left the palace in pomp and wended its way along the roads between ropes stretched to hold back the onlookers. It was the king and his wives on their way to hunt.

The sovereign could also be seen when he went to offer solemn sacrifices, to dispense justice or when he travelled at the head of his troops.

In principle, it was the king who was expected to dispense justice, but as it would have been impossible for him to hear all the cases, he called upon a Brahman to take his place.

There was no proper legal code covering all the problems of social life, but as we shall see from the following quotation which has been taken, like its predecessor, from Manu, established custom usually had the force of law:

"A virtuous king, after studying the special laws for castes and provinces, the regulations for companies of merchants, and family customs, should invest them with the force of law, provided that such laws, regulations and customs do not contradict the principles of the writings revealed to man."

Personal disputes were infrequent. Unlike their predilections nowadays, the Hindus disliked lawsuits. Misdemeanors and crimes were judged with great care and solemnity.

They were often discovered by spies. The system of spying was used both for legal purposes and in politics. Courtesans were the principal agents. From the moment of his arrival in the country, a stranger was

24

surrounded by spies who never left him alone, but whose presence was never suspected by him.

On the other hand, bearing false witness was regarded as one of the most serious crimes. When discovered, it was severely punished in this world and was subject to even more stringent punishment in the next.

The eighth and ninth books of the laws of Manu consist entirely of strictures on the judgement of misdemeanors and crimes and on the sanctions applicable to the guilty persons.

These precepts are addressed directly to the king, who is the chief justice of the State and is responsible for all offenses, petty or serious, committed in it.

The methods used to collect a debt were persuasion, the intervention of friends, constraints imposed on the debtor who was followed everywhere, (even into his house), detention of his wife or children by the creditor, and even a beating.

Facilities were granted to the debtor; he could free himself by working or by paying in instalments. When an arrangement, exchange or sale was concluded, 10 days were allowed in which either party could withdraw. The act did not become irrevocable until the 10-day period had finished.

The interest payable on money was fixed

Left: Pottery from Kashmir (Graeco-Buddhist art). Right: torso of a fairy (Christian era).

by law. It varied according to caste: the Brahman paid less than the Kshatriya who in his turn paid less than a man of low caste.

The punishments inflicted for major crimes such as murder or adultery were confiscation of property, exile or death, while for theft, there were fines, mutilation or imprisonment.

Rape, violence to young girls and adultery were capital crimes because they were liable to mix the castes, which the laws of Manu were specifically intended to prevent.

Among the Brahman Hindus, the army consisted of the entire caste of Kshatriyas. A Kshatriya who followed any other occupation failed in his duty, and he was not authorized to do so by law except in case of extreme necessity. Even in peacetime, the Kshatriyas led a military life.

Megasthenes speaks of the camp which accommodated all the warriors and estimates them to have numbered 400,000. They spent the day in tests of strength and skill, in games, sleeping or drinking. From time to time, the king would hold a review of them.

Megasthenes admired the good order prevailing in that camp of 400,000 men and above all the absolute honesty of the Hindus. Although the soldiers lived at such close quarters, he never heard it said that one of them had stolen anything from another.

While the Hindu writings are in favor of using all the stratagems of war and wiles of diplomacy, they also contain precepts full of compassion such as the prohibition to use arms that make complex and cruel wounds such as poisoned arrows, and to strike an enemy who is temporarily unable to defend himself because he is wounded or is already fighting another adversary.

Generosity towards the vanquished is highly recommended by Manu. It is in fact advocated as sound policy because:

"In acquiring wealth and extending his territory, the king will add to his resources less than by winning over a true friend who, however weak, may one day become powerful."

After a successful expedition, the king could carry off the booty provided that he offered a substantial share to the Brahmans. However, he was recommended, in his own interests, not to despoil the peoples he had subjected.

"To take away valuable objects which may give rise to hate, or to give them away, which inspires friendship, may be praiseworthy or ill-judged according to the circumstances."

A sound recommendation, which recalls the policy of the wisest of rulers—the Romans —counsels the conqueror to respect the laws and the religious beliefs of the people he has subjugated.

Agriculture and commerce were, as we have said, in the hands of the Vaishyas. The people of that caste, however, although they were entitled to own property and to acquire wealth, were not their own masters. Their

Sculpture from the 2nd century B.C.

28

suzerain and the true owner of the land was the king.

All the terms for buying and selling, the price of the goods, the value of the weights and measures, the imports and the exports, were determined in every detail by the king.

"After considering, in the case of all goods, from what distance they come if they are from a foreign country, how far away they must be sent if they are to be exported, how long they have been stored, the profit to be expected and the outlays made on them, the king shall establish regulations for their sale and purchase.

"Every five or fifteen days, depending on how much the price of the goods varies, the king shall regulate their prices in the presence of experts.

"The value of precious metals and the weight and measures shall be precisely specified by him, and every six months he shall review them."

The weights and measures in current use were mainly of gold, copper and silver. The most stringent penalties were imposed on persons who falsified their tax liabilities or the quality of their goods.

"Whosoever evades his obligations, who buys or sells at illegal times or who wrongly assesses his goods shall be fined eight times their value.

"No product shall be mixed with another

Two pillars from railing of Buddhist temple (2nd century A.D.).

and sold as the pure substance nor shall a product of poor quality be sold as sound."

The bulk of the taxes went to cover war expenditures. The Vaishyas were exempt from military service of any kind because they were not of noble enough birth to bear arms. While the Kshatriyas defended the frontiers, the Vaishas cultivated the land in complete safety. In good years, they could amass money and in times of famine they knew that the royal treasury would assist them, since the king was their master and father and would not leave them to perish. They had their local feast days; they were heads of households and took pleasure in the health and prosperity of their families.

They did not lack servants. The laws of Manu number seven kinds of servants who were veritable slaves without the right to possessions of any kind.

"There are seven kinds of servants: the captives taken in battle, the domestic servant who enters the household in order to be maintained, the serf born of a female slave on the estate of her master, the servant who is bought or given away, a servant belonging first to a father and then to his son, and the person who becomes a slave as a punishment or who is unable to pay a fine.

"A wife, a son and a slave are not allowed to hold property themselves under the law. Whatever they acquire becomes the property of the person on whom they depend."

Despite its many and stringent requirements the law still had its human side. Whoever was unable to work was exempt from payment of tax.

"A blind man, a congenital idiot, a cripple, an old man, and a man who assists persons who are well-versed in the holy writings must not be required by the king to pay any tax whatsoever."

The poorest artisans gave one working day a month in lieu of tax.

During the Brahmanic period, a woman was no longer, as in Vedic times, the fiancée sought after and courted by great displays of prowess, or the mistress of the house, dignified and respected, who shared with her husband the honors of the sacrifice. Her role had become much more modest. It is described in the following words by Manu:

"To give birth to children, to raise them after they have come into the world, to take care of the household each day, these are the duties of women."

Again according to Manu, women must be always in a subordinate position, and their lives are to be spent in obedience to their superiors.

"A little girl, a young woman, even an older woman, may not do as she wishes even in her own home.

"A woman is under the guardianship of her father during her childhood, under the guardianship of her husband during her youth, under the guardianship of her children

Fragment of railing from Buddhist temple.

in her old age. She may never do exactly as she wishes."

No sin was more to be chastised than adultery because, as Manu says:

"It is adultery that brings the mixture of castes into the world and from that mixture springs the failure to perform one's duty, which leads to the destruction of the human race and of the world."

The guilty woman and her accomplice were therefore condemned to the most frightful punishments, particularly if the adulterous wife was of high caste.

"If a woman who should be proud of her family and of its caste is unfaithful to her husband, may the King send her to be devoured by dogs in a place that is much frequented.

"He shall condemn the adulterer, her accomplice, to be burnt on a red-hot bed of iron, and the executors shall constantly feed the fire with wood until the sinner has died."

The faithfulness to be expected of a husband towards his wife and his duty to her are specified by the laws of Manu no less precisely than the duties of the wife. Happiness in this world and the future prosperity of the race are based on the perfect union of man and woman in marriage. Many are the recommendations made to a young man to chose a suitable companion, and he may not abandon her later unless she comes to hate him or bears him nothing but daughters.

"She who, although ill, is good and of virtuous conduct, may not be replaced without

Above: detail of medallion from railing of Buddhist temple.

33

her consent and must never be treated unkindly."

The first duty of a husband was to make his wife happy and it was believed, almost superstitiously, that a house in which a woman was ill-treated in any way or was not held in esteem by those in her immediate household was doomed to fall into ruins.

"Wherever women are honored, the gods are satisfied, but when they are not honored, all pious acts become sterile.

"In every family where the husband is content with his wife and the wife with her husband, their happiness is assured for ever.

"Married women should be covered with attentions and gifts by their fathers, their brothers, their husbands, and their husband's brothers if these hope for prosperity."

Marriage was not in any way a business transaction. The father of the young girl could neither give nor receive money. His main concern had to be the virtues of the suitor.

"Even a Shudra", says Manu, "should not be rewarded in any way when he gives his daughter in marriage because the father who receives a reward is in a sense selling his daughter.

"It would be better for a daughter of marriagable age to remain in her father's house to the day of her death than to be given by her father to a husband without virtue."

A family was solidly established, and its members had reciprocal rights and duties.

"They shall be faithful to one another till the day of their death: this is the first duty of

Sculpture from the 6th century (National Museum, Delhi).

34

Left: Brahma, creator of the world (Paris, Musée Guimet). Right: Brahma and Krishna (id.).

the wife and the husband.

"The loving duties of the man and his wife are hereby proclaimed."

The custom of burning the widow alive on the funeral pyre of her husband, which has only recently been stamped out in India, is not mentioned in the laws of Manu. It must already have begun to gain ground though because it is spoken of by the Greek historians of the Macedonian conquest.

Although Buddhism already existed at the beginning of the period which we are now considering, it had not yet become very prominent.

Megasthenes talks of Buddhist monks with their new doctrines, which were causing something of a stir in his day, as well as the opposition they encountered from the Brahmans. Yet Buddhism did not become the official religion of India until some time later, until the reign of Ashoka, two and a half centuries before the birth of Christ.

This chapter is hardly the place for a detailed analysis of the old Brahman theology, with all the intricate details of its rites and sacrifices. Here we can merely indicate the most widespread new philosophical trends. These are clearly summarized in the book of Manu, which simply repeats in more precise language the rather diffuse content of the Brahmanas and the Upanishads.

The rather nebulous gods of the Rig Veda, which were not to assume the distinct forms of Shiva and Vishnu until much later, now became even more nebulous than they had

been when the Vedas were written. They are cold abstract manifestations of Brahma, the supreme principle, the spirit which animates all living beings. However, this Brahma is no longer the sovereign lord one sees in the pages of the Vedas as the creator of all things and beings, able to impose his will upon all. Far from controlling the world, he is now not even independent of it. He is scattered among all creatures, from the most noble to the most base, sharing their existence and fated to remain with them throughout the long sequence of their faults, sufferings, rebirths, and their slow, laborious strivings towards perfection.

According to Manu, the supreme soul resides in beings of both the highest and the lowest orders.

"The substance of that supreme soul emits countless vital principles, like sparks from a fire, which constantly impart movement to the creatures of the various orders."

Since, in this dogma, Man recognizes the supreme Soul in any manifestation of life, he must respect the lives of all beings, even of pests and the frailest insects.

"In this way, the man who recognizes in his own soul the supreme soul which is present in all creatures, treats all beings equally and achieves the highest destiny, that of being finally absorbed into Brahma.

"If a Brahman cannot, by offering gifts,

Incarnation of Vishnu (wood from a chariot).

expiate the error he has committed in killing a snake or some other creature, he must do penance each time in order to atone for his sin.

"If he has killed a thousand small animals with bones or enough animals without bones to fill a chariot, he shall perform the same penance as for the killing of a Shudra."

The soul is not conceived of separately from the idea of God. In any animate being, it is a portion of the supreme principle. The sum total of all the individual souls of gods, men and animals constitutes the Supreme Soul, the multiple and also impersonal God whence flow all acts, all life and all change.

"The soul is the sum of all of the gods; the universe resides in the supreme soul; it is the soul which produces the series of acts performed by animate beings."

This sovereign master of the world is a being which no imagination can possibly visualize—he is a non-material, irresistible principle, animating the universe within which he moves, just like the earlier Agni of the Aryans, the omnipotent and ubiquitous fire which the Brahman, trembling with awe, used to feel circulating through his own veins. The Code of Manu has this to say on the subject:

"The great Being must be thought of as the sovereign master of the universe, as more subtle than an atom and brighter than the purest gold; this is a Being which the mind can conceive of only in the sleep of the most abstract contemplation.

"Some worship it in the elemental fire, others in Manu, the lord of creatures, others in Indra,

39

others in the air, others in the eternal Brahma.

"It is this God who, wrapping all beings in a body formed of the five elements, leads them successively from birth to growth, from growth to dissolution, in a motion similar to that of a wheel."

In fact, this is pantheism; but it is no longer the strikingly material and visible pantheism of the Aryans, in which the forces of nature become divine, yet remain clothed in clouds and sunbeams, and keep the scent of their breath and the tenderness or loudness of their voices. This pantheism is more abstract and more fatalistic: the splendid shapes and bright colors no longer show God, they now hide him; he is there, under the elements, but is, as it were, imprisoned. His true glory lies in his lack of form, appearance, will and life: all those who have expiated their sins will become like him, or will be absorbed into him.

Before reaching this state of final beatitude, man has to endure a life which must seem frighteningly long to the Hindu's fertile imagination. A single human lifespan is nothing; a child coming into the world has already passed through many earlier states, and an old man on the point of death has yet to experience childhood and old age many times again, in many different bodies.

Manu gives a clear account of the principle of the transmigration of souls, a fundamental dogma of all the religious sects of India, in-

Medallion from railing of Buddhist temple. (Archeological Museum, Amaravati).

cluding Buddhism, and of another principle common to all later Indian religious sects, the doctrine of Karma, according to which man's conduct in this life determines the state in which he will be reborn.

The relatively good or bad quality of a life determines whether the next life will be of noble or low status, the soul accordingly going to a Brahman, saint or god, or a Chandala (offspring of a union between a male from a high caste and a Sudra—ranked even below the Sudras), the lowest of men, a cow, a pig or a snake.

The various acts a man may have committed at the end of his life, a death-bed repentance, for example, which count for a great deal in Christianity, are not what decides a man's future state: rather, it is the sum of the acts of a whole lifetime, each tiny act contributing to the eventual outcome of this awesome reckoning.

"Every thought, word or deed, good or bad, will bear good or bad fruit accordingly; a man's higher, middle or lower state is the result of his actions."

A consequence of this dogma is the terrible discipline to which the Hindu is subjected, and which denies him freedom of choice in performing the most apparently insignificant acts, even in satisfying his most ordinary bodily needs.

The slightest negligence has its distant penalty which one cannot hope to avoid except by performing immediately all the purification rites which may expunge the fault

committed.

The laws of Manu contain a set of severe injunctions which give some idea of the sheer weight of the restrictions which the Hindus had to endure, and which affected every minute detail of their everyday lives during this period; it contrasts sharply with the broad and easy-going morality of the Aryans of Vedic times.

Times certainly had changed: the free, happy people of an earlier age had become a fearful herd, driven onwards relentlessly, living lives of fear and pain.

The main features of this earlier Brahman society re-appear in neo-Brahman society, made milder, however, by the benevolent influence of Buddhism.

Clearly, relief of some sort was needed from early Brahmanism's crushing grip on men's souls. Harsh restraints hung heavily over the slightest act a man might commit, oppressing both mind and imagination, which now saw gloom and horror everywhere. Everything, except nothingness, was bad. Only the torments described in Dante's Inferno can convey any idea of the horrors which early Brahmans saw all around them, and which they thought would continue to grow worse over fantastically long stretches of time after death, until they had made man fit to be finally absorbed into the universe—in other words, into nothingness. The overwhelming desire for relief which these oppressed masses felt was bound to lead to its own remedy. Some time later, and for very different reasons,

41

this same state of affairs came about in the Roman world: and it was then that Christ appeared.

Asia, too, was about to acclaim a liberator whose gentle and long-awaited message was to resound far and wide in men's souls. Millions of beings were bent double under the yoke of the caste-system, sorely bruised by the shackles of the religious laws, and faced with a hopeless future full of inevitable and ever-lasting torment. Yet, on hearing his words, they were to feel a new breath of love and compassion pass over them. The liberator was Buddha Sakya-Muni, and the good news which he brought to the world was the Buddhist religion.

A couple (5th century).

3. The Buddhist Period

The Buddhist period lasted about a thousand years, from the 3rd century B.C. to the 7th century A.D. During this period, the religion of India was transformed and superb monuments spread all over the peninsula. The remains of these monuments and some recently discovered religious writings make it possible to follow the development of Hindu civilization about this time.

The multitude of inscriptions which king Ashoka left all over his vast domains, about two and a half centuries before Christ, show that profound changes were occurring within the old Brahman world. The laws of Manu depict a society which, for generations, had been under the yoke of a rigid, minutely-detailed religious code of conduct. Extreme anguish must have been the common everyday experience of men who knew that the slightest error of the heart or the senses would bring a dreadful atonement. Moreover, the formidable caste barriers prevented them from even being able to endure this misery together; nor were they able to accept a glass of water from one of their fellows or to offer a word of kindness and hope without committing a crime which would be followed by a long expiation.

But now a fresh wind was beginning to blow over men, bringing pity and kindness to them: their chains fell, their hearts opened up, and the whole face of the old world was going to change. With the coming of the great reformer, a law of charity and love was established, embracing all things and creating a bond between the castes, and all living things.

Our knowledge of the life of the famous reformer, whose name and memory are still sacred to 500 million people, has come down to us clad in the poetic fictions imparted by the legends. Any attempt to reconstruct his life must be based on those legends. The oldest of them, and the one which we shall use to retrace Buddha's life, is the Lalita Vistara, composed in Nepal probably soon after the birth of Christ.

Modern writers have strongly criticized the legendary history of Buddha, pointing with some justification to the fictitious nature of the cycle which the Buddha legend represents, and showing how Sakya-Muni drew on earlier traditions borrowed from Vishnu and Krishna. Much of the history of the Buddha legends is little more than an adaptation of older myths. Even the Buddhist religion itself may be regarded as a selection made among a vast mass of dogmas and practices already in existence.

We do not really need to learn about Buddha's real life. After all, with the possible exception of Mohammed, our knowledge of the lives of most founders of religions is rather imprecise. Their biographies were usually written long after their death. What we do need to know is the real or fictitious Buddha who has been worshipped by so many millions of men for more than twenty centuries.

Although Buddha's religion really made its first appearance in the third century B.C., the reformer himself was born two centuries earlier, in Kapilavastu in southern Nepal.

43

There are several striking points of similarity between the legends about his life and various passages in the Gospels. Like Christ, Buddha was born of a virgin, and his coming was miraculously foretold. Buddha, whose real name was Gautama Sakya-Muni, was of royal stock, just as Jesus was of the house of David. But the childhood and youth of the two reformers were quite different, Gautama being raised as the heir to a throne, whereas the son of Mary worked with Joseph the carpenter. Christ's fast in the desert, after which he was tempted three times by the evil spirit, is extraordinarily similar in every detail to the fast and triple temptation of Sakya-Muni in the solitude of the jungles; a certain episode in which the Hindu sage meets a poor woman and asks her for something to drink reminds one strongly of Christ's famous conversation with the Samaritan woman.

Common features such as these cannot be dismissed lightly, especially when one remembers that the two religions are even closer in substance than in form. Both preach charity, equality and renunciation; both ascribe blame for a man's intentions quite as much as for his actual deeds; both have given rise to monastic orders; both have won the souls of millions of men, in the same spirit and using the same means. One regenerated the East, the other the West. Both reflect the same aspi-

Bas-relief: the birth of Buddha (Graeco-Buddhist art).

rations of mankind, and are merely two different aspects of the same capital event in the moral history of mankind. Whether one owes something to the other or whether each came into being quite independently is of little concern to us here.

In his father's palace, the young Gautama had always enjoyed all the benefits which power, wealth, beauty, health and youth could bestow. On reaching the age of manhood, he had married a beautiful girl whom he adored, and who had just borne him a son. Then, one day, at the peak of his happiness, three events took place which were to decide his destiny: in the same day, he met a sick old man who was hobbling along, bent with age; then a man stricken with the plague, writhing horribly in the most dreadful pain; lastly he came across a pale, disfigured corpse, which the two parents, overcome with grief, were taking for burial.

Gautama asked himself: "What is the reason for old age, sickness and death?"

"I am rich, powerful, happy and strong", he went on. "Yet in spite of wealth and my power, my face will one day become hideously wrinkled, my hair will turn grey, my limbs will be racked by pain and my loved ones will weep over my grave. Since I know what awaits me, how can I possibly enjoy my treasures, my health, my beautiful young wife and my child? Yet I have as much happiness as any man could hope for; what must it be like for the masses of people who have to toil, who are poor, despised and hungry?"

These thoughts led him to the conclusion that the world was nothing but one immense mass of suffering.

"But where does suffering come from?" he wondered. "What causes it? What can be done about it?"

At this point, Buddha was filled with an irresistible desire to discover the sources of the suffering which is inseparable from all life, and to find a remedy for it. Feeling that he could no longer be happy, because he knew that his happiness would have to end, and that even the ephemeral happiness which he did enjoy was only a splendid exception, he left his cherished wife, his newborn son, his aging father, his palace, servants and treasures, put on the clothes of the poor, and, carrying the begging-cup of the mendicant holy-men, he went walking from village to village, living on charity, contemplating life in all its aspects and continuing with his series of meditations.

Finding that his meditations had not yet led him to the solution he was seeking, he isolated himself from the rest of men, went deep into the remotest jungles and devoted his days and nights to thought.

But the years went by, and the mysterious end which he was pursuing still eluded him. All the hardships which he had inflicted on his mind and body had been in vain; he had fasted to the point of losing consciousness and being thought dead; he had immersed himself in the most abstract reasoning about the nature and purpose of things—but all to no avail. He had not yet reached the state of Buddha, which was to turn him into a higher being, capable of illuminating and comforting mankind.

While he was struggling painfully towards supreme knowledge, and was indeed on the point of actually achieving it, he experienced the terrible temptation with which Mara, the evil spirit, prince of demons, tried to thwart his efforts and reduce this wise, holy man to the ranks of sinners.

His mind was troubled by weird visions, which are described in sinister detail in the Lalita Vistara.

First, while he was in the silence of the desert, whole legions of evil spirits swarmed around him, whispering words of doubt in his ear, asking him the eternal question, which can plunge even the hardiest souls into the depths of apathy—"What is it all for?" He was surrounded by an army of demons with flaming-red, livid and black bodies, whose deformed, sunken eyes were bloody, protruding or squinting; there were monsters crowned with wreaths made of men's fingers, headless monsters and monsters with a hundred thousand heads. Yet, by his firm words, he repelled them all. Then, suddenly, the forest was lit with a mysterious glow and became cool as though a rainstorm had just passed. This time, the temptation took a seductive form. The sage now found his meditations interrupted by a swirling mass of Apsaras, the daughters of the evil spirits. Exquisite shapes floated from branch to branch and wound themselves around each

An apsaras, or nymph (Sandstone, 6th century).

other voluptuously. He was surrounded by provocative women and modest women, by lavishly dressed women and women revealing their magnificent nude bodies, some with flashing eyes under long eyelashes, others looking up at him longingly and tenderly. All of them sought to move him with words of love, lascivious poses or promises of untold pleasures.

But Sakya-Muni, bolstering his resistance to these enchanting temptresses, replied, again according to the legend:

"I see the body as unclean and impure, filled with families of worms, consumed by fire, fragile and overwhelmed with suffering. I shall achieve the everlasting dignity revered by wise men, which is the highest happiness in the world of living and inanimate things."

Yet the tender voice went on: "After showing you the 64 spirits of desire they have shaken their belts and their legs, making the sound of bells, they have laughed and danced excitedly before you: is this a reason to disdain them? What wrong have they done to you?"

But Shakya-Muni, withstanding this temptation, replied:

"All creatures have sin within them; and he who unleashed this display of passion for me to see was well aware of it. Desire is like a sword, a dart, a sting; it is like a razor with honey on its edge, the head of a serpent and a trench of fire; this is how I see desire."

At this point, the chief demon himself came, as Satan had done to Christ, to show the future Buddha all the kingdoms of the world and their glory, promising him success,

47

triumph and power, if he gave up his quest for wisdom.

The demon said: "I am the lord of desire throughout the whole world; gods, men and beasts are all under my power and move only at my will. You, too, are in my domain; arise and speak."

"If you are the lord of desire", replied Shakya-Muni, "you are not the lord of the visible world. Look at me, for I am the lord of the law. If you are the lord of desire, do not follow the wrong path. I shall attain understanding in spite of you and within your sight."

Abandoning the struggle, the fearsome army of demons vanished into the darkness, with cries of rage. Shakya-Muni had triumphed. A cool rain of flowers fell over him, and a heavenly voice was heard saying:

"The gods offer you garlands of pearls, standards and banners; they will cause flowers and sandalwood powder to rain as these words are said: Oh great hero, the enemy and his troops, who had surrounded your tree, have been vanquished."

The tree referred to in this passage is the one Sakya-Muni had stood under in his solitude. It was situated in the place now known as Buddh-Gaya. It is venerated to this day, just like the olive-trees of Gethsemane, in the shadow of which Jesus felt the bloody sweat

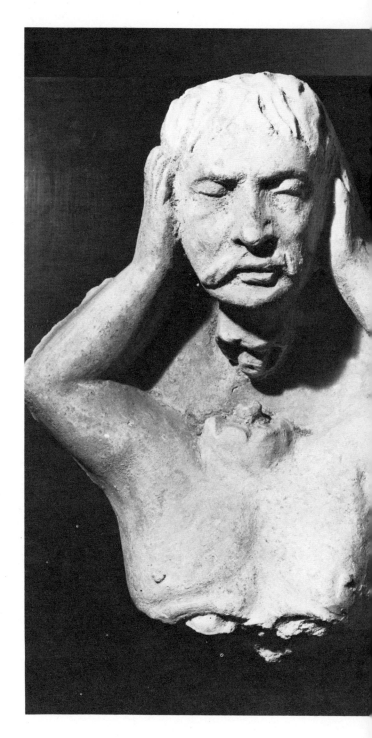

Demon tearing off its head (Paris, Musée Guimet).

pour down his brow. The branches which sheltered the Buddha have long since been reduced to dust, but the piety of the faithful has always replaced the tree when it came to the end of its days.

As soon as he had overcome the temptation, the wise man, now in possession of supreme knowledge, achieved the solution of the awesome problems which he had set himself.

Tracing it back through a sequence of causes and effects, he recognized that the foundation of all evil is desire, and its pinnacle is illusion. The desire which takes possession of a man from the day he is born devours his heart like a hydra which is never satisfied and perpetually renews itself. Any food tossed to it, such as glory, power, wealth, honors, sen-

suous delights, pleasures of the mind, youth, beauty and love, are nothing more than fleeting forms and deceptive illusions. Man aspires to everything, and nothing exists but vain phantoms. Since everything in the universe is constantly changing, and since all beings and things are destroyed and renewed, not remaining the same for one single day, what does exist then, other than the illusions created and pursued by unceasing desire? This being so, how could we do better than to kill that desire within us, thereby destroying illusion and, consequently, suffering?

The annihilation of all desire, detachment from the things of this world, and, ultimately, the destruction of form and illusion, leading to the state of Nirvana, in which consciousness

Ruins near Benares; Buddha delivered his first sermon here.

and even thought disappear, were all embodied in the doctrine preached by Sakya-Muni when he eventually rose from where he had been sitting under the tree of wisdom and returned to his fellow-men.

If Sakya-Muni had brought the world nothing but the philosophical abstractions attributed to him by the legends, his name would never have emerged from the dusty obscurity of thousands of generations. After all, mere philosophical reasoning has never moved the masses. Only the voice of feeling has any effect on them. Anyone who would make an impression on men must share their aspirations and sufferings, and also move their hearts.

Buddha's prodigious success was due pre-cisely to his ability to move men. This royal prince had become a beggar of his own accord, so as to share the wretched plight of the masses and to teach them how to free themselves from it; he thus endeared himself to the people. Like Christ, Buddha understood and shared men's grief, and taught them the value of charity and hope. This is why he still has such power over men's minds.

Strictly speaking, Buddhism did not give the world a new religion, but rather a new morality. As for dogmas, it had only one, and that consisted of an affirmation of illusion and nothingness.

In actual fact, it overthrew nothing and fought nothing. It allowed Brahmanism to remain in existence, with its gods and castes.

The only difference was that gods and demons, Brahmans and Shudras, were now mere ephemeral forms, subject to constant change, and passing through the state of Buddha to reach the supreme nothingness. Becoming Buddha means possessing absolute intelligence, being able to see in a flash the long sequence of earlier existences, the purpose of life, the long chain of cause and effect, and then entering into the supreme eternal peace of Nirvana: this was the goal towards which all living things—plants, animals, gods and men—moved, through countless transmigrations and incarnations.

As nature had existed since the beginning of time, and was the essence of all things, it was regarded as a boundless nothingness, an unconscionable void. Occasionally, however, this void could undergo the fatal effect of desire and assume a form, becoming capable of feeling, awareness and acts of the will—in short, it could come alive. At this point, the series of transformations begins. The now incarnate principle, henceforth able to perform good or bad acts, could not recover its original tranquil essence except through the merit of its acts. Its elevation from a lower to a higher state was determined by the Karma, that is, by the whole outcome of all of its deeds, words and thoughts throughout one of its lives. It

Left: Buddha-Gaya, cradle of Buddhism. Opposite: detail of a statue of Buddha preaching (Graeco-Buddhist style).

51

moved through the stages of man, then of a religious, then to the state of Bodhisattva and, lastly, having become Buddha, it fell back into the eternally tranquil, silent abyss from which desire had called it forth. As long as it remained alive, it had been accompanied by that desire, which had brought with it a whole procession of sufferings. Each true Buddhist sought, then, to annihilate desire within himself, in order to attain supreme repose as quickly as possible.

This constant striving is accompanied by good deeds, performed with the same end in mind. All deeds, whether actual or intended, whether spoken or thought, all bear fruit: all of them count, without exception.

This was a religious reform which raised up the wretches oppressed by the caste system, and which made them, in theory if not politically, equal to their arrogant masters in their nature and in the future which lay ahead of them; it was a reform which brought kind words and gentle precepts into a society which was held down by a rule of iron; it was a reform which proclaimed, above all, its ability to point to the causes of suffering, to trace it back to its origins and to give the means of destroying it to a race of men which had grown weak from the extreme climate, and which was as terrified by the nightmares of a savage religion as it was by the sudden fury of the implacable elements. Clearly, a reform such as this stood a very good chance of success. It had grown out of certain obvious needs and was designed to meet those needs.

Buddha preaching (National Museum, Delhi).

Left: an ascetic, in the "Yogasana" pose. Right: a Gautama ascetic in meditation.

55

In addition to these spiritual causes, the propagation of Buddhism in India received some material assistance as well. The whole of the northern part of the peninsula, Hindustan in fact, became united in a single empire under Ashoka, two and a half centuries before Christ. In an absolute monarchy, once the sovereign adopts a religion, it instantly flourishes and spreads. This is what happened to Christianity in the Roman Empire when Constantine became a convert. A number of authors have quite rightly called Ashoka the Buddhist Constantine of India.

The precious documents which he left, in the form of inscriptions carved on columns and rock faces all over his empire show how zealously he set about propagating the new doctrines. They also make it clear that the prompt acceptance of these doctrines by everyone, from the ignorant to the wise, from the Pariahs to the Brahmans, was due to their most accessible and popular aspect, that is, to their benign morality and their spirit of charity.

Buddhism gradually became an established religion, with its gods, ceremonies, forms of worship and its philosophy. Its definitive triumph was impeded, however, by its lack of divinities. Unable to offer the masses any particular divinities of its own, yet at the same time compelled to indulge the popular craving for them, it allowed all the Brahman gods to survive. It is true that Buddhism did declare them to be far beneath the religious man, and particularly so in the case of a man who

had reached the state of Buddha. Yet, in the minds of the superstitious masses, the great multitude of these gods kept most of their former status, and eventually overwhelmed and absorbed Buddhism, forcing it to merge with Brahmanism. This explains why the country of its birth was precisely the country where it vanished forever.

Buddhist sects soon grew in number, as the Brahman sects had done before them; nevertheless, although in the temple Buddha was soon reduced to the rank of quite an ordinary god, whose features were gradually fixed by legend, he did become, for some sects, a higher state to which all creatures aspired, and which they eventually attained through their own merits after thousands of rebirths and vast tracts of time.

In the view of the new sects, the Buddha Sakya-Muni was not the only one who was to bring the truth to the world. Someone else would come, to be followed by someone else, bringing new illumination, new strength and showing quicker ways to perfection. However, the emergence of these figures was to be separated by fantastic numbers of centuries, since the formation of a Buddha takes a very long time, and the Hindu imagination, which is quite unperturbable, used to accumulate whole series of *kalpas,* even one of which far surpasses our modest Western ways of thinking.

The best preparation for the state of Buddha is the ascetic state, which accounts for the monastic system which soon led to the appear-

Coffin of Buddha (Graeco-Buddhist style).

ance of numerous monasteries, dotted all over the Indian landscape.

In addition to the desire to overcome suffering and to attain the glorious state of Buddha, followed by perfect repose, there was another reason why large numbers of disciples rushed to the seclusion of the monastic life: it was because equality, a principle proclaimed by Buddha, did in fact prevail in the depths of the monasteries. In them, Sudras, Pariahs and Chandalas were all equal to the Brahman and all ate at the same table once they had joined the same holy congregation. Women had their own convents, and ceased to be the weak creatures whom Manu described as being subject to constant guardianship.

India built these monasteries, hewn out of the mountainsides, over a span of one thousand years; they are still architectural marvels to this day. Life inside them, however, was quite severe: those seeking admission had to take vows of poverty and chastity, and leave behind them wives, children and wealth in order to devote themselves to a new existence. Having no possessions, the monks were expected to live on alms, but without actually asking for them, and to accept from charitable donors only enough to provide for a meal.

They had to teach peace and truth to men, to found hospitals and places of rest for travellers and the poor, to try to prevent wars, and to profess the greatest tolerance for all other religions, since they were to be thought of as inferior forms of the same truth.

In the centuries which followed, Buddha had millions of disciples from the most obscure segments of the population, from among the ignorant, the insignificant and the downtrodden. They flocked to his temples, proud to be standing next to the arrogant Brahmans, prostrated themselves before his divine image, worshipped his relics and celebrated the solemn festivals in honor of his begging-cup. Their understanding of him did not go beyond his gentle charity: their fondest recollection was that when one of Buddha's companions asked a woman from the lowest levels of society for water to drink, she had humbly replied, aware that a man of his caste would sooner die than knowingly accept a drop of water from the hand of a person like her: "Master, I am a Chandala". The gentle reply was: "I am not asking you if you are a Chandala; I am thirsty and would like you to give me something to drink."

This incident may not seem very significant in itself, but for a Hindu it was a miracle

Buddha preaching. Right: remains of a temple in Kashmir, and decorations of the façade of a temple at Bhubanesvara (8th century).

of charity and signalled a profound uplift for vast numbers of human beings.

So much for Buddhism; even though its philosophy later strayed into abstractions bordering on hallucinations, and its mode of worship became submerged among numerous Brahman rituals, ceremonies and symbols, it was, nonetheless, by virtue of its profound kindness, destined to become a powerful and effective force for renewal, without equal in the history of mankind.

One should not forget, of course, that this disappearance, or rather transformation, which we have covered in a matter of a few lines, took about a thousand years.

The numerous monuments which give an account of its history were built between the third century B.C. and the 3rd century A.D. Throughout this long period, Buddha was at all times worshipped as an omnipotent god by his faithful. In the legends, he appears to his disciples and grants them favors. The pilgrim Hiouen Thsang, who, having spent a long time being initiated into Buddhism in India, was one of the most ardent followers of Buddha, told how Buddha appeared to him in a cave, when he visited the peninsula in the 7th century A.D.

The rest is well known. After spreading from India to the rest of Asia, having invaded China, Tartary, Burma, etc., Buddhism, which is now the religion of 800 million people, vanished almost entirely from the country of its birth in about the 7th or 8th centuries A.D. It is still to be found in India, but only at

60

the outer edges of this vast empire: in Nepal in the north, and Ceylon in the south. Since Hindu literature is silent on this point, it has been argued that violent persecutions accounted for its disappearance. Even if one were to concede that the tolerance of the Hindu character could be compatible with the idea of religious persecutions and that persecution destroys religions instead of propagating them, as history tells us, even if one were to agree to these highly unlikely hypotheses, one difficulty would still remain. It is this: why, in a country divided, as India then was, into a hundred or so small kingdoms, should all the princes simultaneously and abruptly decide to abandon the religion practised by their ancestors for generations, and compel their subjects to adopt a new religion?

A study of the monuments of India immediately suggests a reason for the transformation of Buddhism, and shows how erroneous earlier explanations have been. After carefully studying most of the important monuments of India, one has to conclude that Buddhism disappeared quite simply because it gradually merged with the religion which had given it birth.

Theses changes happened very slowly; but in a country like India where there is no history as such, and where one sometimes comes across periods of 5 or 6 centuries about which we know absolutely nothing, there is often no way of joining up a sudden change with the period just preceding it.

When one scrutinizes the statues and bas-reliefs with which Indian monuments are covered, the history of the transformation of Buddhism becomes quite clear. These monuments show how the founder of the religion which disdained all gods actually became a god himself, and, though he did not appear, initially, in any temples at all, he could eventually be found in all of them. He can be seen gradually merging with the ancient Brahman gods, until he who had once towered above the multitude of other gods, ended up as an accessory deity, and was lost in the crowd.

A number of philosophical sects, like those of the Brahminic period, grew up alongside Buddhism. Their doctrines contain no new ideas; but since some of their works have been translated into certain European languages and have been mistaken for Buddhist ideas, a brief account of their general spirit might not be out of place.

Basically, they proclaim the universal vanity of things, on earth and in heaven. All beings are mere appearances, phenomena in the process of disappearing, like the foam which bubbles for an instant on the surface of the sea. "There are neither men nor women nor creation nor life nor anyone: these conditions are entirely unreal, figments of the imagination. They are all like a dream; they are like the moon reflected in the water."

Fragment of a mask of Buddha, of Afghan origin (Paris, Musée Guimet).

61

In this philosophical doctrine, which goes well beyond anything thought of by Europeans, there is no god who existed before the world and created it. Nature is an infinite chain—stretching infinitely ahead and behind—of birth and destruction, of perpetual decomposition and recomposition, of causes which are effects and effects which are causes, of phenomena without beginning or end.

Having suppressed the idea of creation, the Buddhist philosophers also suppressed the fatalistic conception of destiny which dominates all the Hellenic religions. No destiny governs the life of things; the future destiny of each creature is governed solely by its conduct. Events are connected by the moral law. Only acts, or at least the consequences of those acts, are eternal. By one's own merits, it is possible, after a long series of rebirths, to achieve the supreme good of non-being and become insensitive to tears and grief, entering into Nirvana, after which it is no longer necessary to put on new forms.

On this serene region to which the Buddhist has risen, "the name of Buddha is a mere word, and Buddha himself is like an illusion or a dream".

Anyone seeking an illustration of the benign influence which Buddhist morality had on society could do no better than study the edicts of Ashoka, which are full of precepts calling for concord, peace and charity among men.

These edicts differ from the laws of Manu in three basic ways: universal good-will applying even to animals and including a prohibition of the killing of animals; a spirit of equality which called upon all castes to listen to religious preaching and to heed its promises; religious tolerance—the many religious sects were felt to be varied manifestations of mankind's striving towards the absolute ideal and were, therefore, worthy of respect.

In Brahman society, animals were shown a certain deference since they were also, to some extent, animated by the supreme spirit, and were held to represent the forms in which man's sins often condemned him to be reborn. Yet people used to kill them without too much soul-searching. Hunting was a major pastime of the kings and Kshatriyas, and bloody sacrifices were common. Ashoka put an end to all of that.

He decreed measures for the benefit of man and, at the same time, of animals.

"Grasses useful to man and those useful to animals will be taken and planted in places where they do not grow naturally; the same shall be done with fruit trees; all along the public highway, trees shall be planted and wells dug for the benefit of men and animals."

In primitive Brahmanism, the "twice-born men", that is, those of the first three castes, were the only ones privileged to enjoy the benefits of religion, and to hear its teaching. Any Sudra found listening to the preaching of a Brahman or the reading of the sacred scriptures was to have his ears filled with boiling oil.

"Ministers of religion shall go forth to preach to the warriors, the Brahmans, beggars, the destitute and others, without any impediment, for the joy of those who are already well disposed, in order to set free those who are in bonds and to restore the freedom of those who are prisoners."

Buddhism does not seem to have remained a state religion for very long, as it had been under Ashoka. Only a century after this prince, a number of his successors had reverted to Brahmanism. Nevertheless, the new religion was to remain dominant and popular for six or seven centuries. It was still flourishing in 399-414 A.D., when the Chinese pilgrim Fa-Hian visited India. Two centuries later, Hiouen-Thsang, who followed him, saw the decadence into which Buddhism had fallen, its temples and monasteries everywhere abandoned and in ruins. About a thousand years after Asoka, Buddhism had disappeared from India, as Brahmanism had triumphed completely. Yet it was not to disappear as a moral principle. Its influence can still be felt today, as it gave rise to neo-Brahmanism, the present religion of the Hindus.

Hunters. Frieze from a temple at Khajurao (10th century).

4. The Neo-Brahman Period

This period begins about the 8th century A.D., at a time when Buddhism had almost completely vanished. The death of the old religion produced some very palpable changes in society. Buddhism was replaced by an old-style Brahmanism which had itself been profoundly changed by the form of worship which it was replacing.

India had become divided into many small kingdoms with absolute monarchies, each of them independent and usually in competition with each other.

From a purely historical point of view, this period, from the 8th to the 12th century, from the disappearance of Buddhism up to the time of the Moslem invasions, is rather obscure. If it were not for the monuments which describe the splendor of the kingdoms which flourished at that time, we would know very little indeed. Ruined buildings, a few rare inscriptions, some coins and a few literary works entirely lacking in any chronology are all that has come down to us from that period. Yet even these are enough to tell us that this new age was no less brilliant than the preceding one.

There are grounds for considering the Hindu civilization of the time as more or less comparable to the late Middle Ages in Europe. The arts were certainly well developed; the superb monuments of Khajurao, Mount Abu, etc., are definitely the equals of our finest examples of Gothic art; outstanding works such as these could be produced only in a rich, sophisticated society which encouraged the arts and had many great artists.

The literature—both drama and poetry—is also remarkable, but is not too reliable for our purposes, since it is often difficult to place these works in time; sometimes the margin of error is as much as seven or eight centuries.

A description of a major Hindu city and of Hindu society can be found in the remarkable drama by Shudraka, "The Little Clay Cart". The action takes place in Ojein, capital of Malwa, which is now in ruins. Such is the splendor of the palaces, houses and temples which it describes that the reader is immediately reminded of Gwalior, Khajurao and Mount Abu. The author depicts a fairyland of marble palaces inlaid with precious stones, their halls adorned with golden panels studded with diamonds and graced with arches made of carved ivory, their outer walls surrounded by gardens full of the brightest flowers and refreshing shade trees; he talks of majestic temples reflected in the waters of the river, containing mysterious sanctuaries in which unveiled priestesses dance before the gods to the harmonious sound of the tiny bells on the gold and silver rings which adorn their ankles and arms.

One of the most sumptuous dwellings in the city is that of Vasantasana, the great hetaira, an exceedingly prominent citizen,

Sculptures in the temple of Kandariya, the largest of the temples at Khajurao.

because in those days hetairas played as important a role as they did in the Greek society of Pericles' day. By comparison, the luxury enjoyed by the richest of modern courtesans seems mild indeed.

Eight different courtyards, covered in elegant mosaics, dazzling carpets, arches inlaid with ivory and draped with flags, columns bearing crystal vases, panels of shining gold, painted pavilions, marble staircases, banisters laced with strings of pearls; in the stables, bulls, oxen, rams, horses, monkeys and elephants; gaming-tables for the élite of the libertines of Ojein; a host of assorted musicians, singers, dancers, actors, readers, all in the service of the mistress of the house; huge kitchens, constantly in operation which gave the glutton Metreya a taste of the paradise of Indra; perfumery stalls and jewellers' workshop, all subordinate to the house, imparted a bazaar-like atmosphere; a swarm of servants and hangers-on chattered and laughed among themselves, chewing musc or betel-leaves and drinking strong spirits; there were bowls of saffron water; parrots, jays, cuckoos, partridges, quails, peacocks and swans could be seen through the bars of huge gilded aviaries; outside, there was a lush green garden with swings hanging from silken ropes.

As it was in the time of Megasthenes, and as it still is today, the society we find at Ojein

is based on the caste system. The professions were hereditary, and were arranged according to a complex hierarchy, but with Brahmans invariably at the top. Some of these were ascetics, but others lived gay, elegant lives devoted to the pursuit of pleasure and pretty women, though, curiously enough, such a lifestyle did not seem to diminish the esteem in which they were held.

As one might expect, the sovereign was always an absolute monarch whose supreme power was tempered only by the conspiracies which constantly threatened him, and from which the Kshatriyas surrounding him could not always protect him.

Justice seemed to be done more or less fairly, unless one of the parties involved happened to be an important person, in which case his power prevailed.

The prologue, written some time after the play, lists the kinds of knowledge which were most highly prized: a king is praised for his knowledge of the Vedas, mathematics and the fine arts, and also his talent for raising elephants.

We can form a fairly clear idea of the daily activities of a king, if not from the preceding drama, at least from other Hindu narratives of the period, in particular the "32 tales of the enchanted throne". It can be safely assumed that this would also show us how the great lords behaved, as they would naturally tend to imitate the king.

Awakened in the morning by musical instruments, he first performed his religious

12th-century sculptures, at Chidarmbaram.

practices and acts of charity. Then, after a few moments devoted to improving his skill in the use of arms, he assembled his ministers and dispatched his business.

About noon, he ate a meal preceded by religious invocations, and followed by a siesta. He then strolled through the shaded gardens of the palace, surrounded by his wives and dancing-girls, picking flowers, singing, and being pushed on swings with silken cords.

More religious acts were performed in the evening, followed by a meal and entertainments—singing, dancing and music—up until the time when the sovereign withdrew into the harem.

According to "The Earthenware Chariot", the official religion of the city of Ojein was Brahmanism. Buddhism still existed, but does not seem to have been much more than the sect of religious mendicants.

5. The Hindu-Moslem Period

The Moslem period of the history of India began in the 11th century and lasted, at least politically, until the 18th. Thanks to the Moslem historians, more is known about this period than about any of those that preceded it.

During the 700 years of Moslem rule, India was more or less completely subjugated to conquerors of different races: Arabs, Turks, Afghans and Moghuls, all of whom, however, professed the religion of Mohammed and his successors.

These conquerors caused profound changes in the language, beliefs and arts of India, changes which can be said to have lasted until today, since 50 million people on the Indian subcontinent now follow the law of the Koran, and, over much of the peninsula, a language is spoken which derives largely from that of its former masters.

The new civilization which the Afghans, and later the Turks and the Moghuls, brought to the Indus and Ganges basin strongly influenced the one already existing there, and was, in turn, modified by it. The mixture of these two civilizations gave birth to a third, almost equally indebted to both of them, which we shall call the Hindu-Moslem civilization.

When they reached India, the Moghuls had already conquered most of Asia and had threatened Europe. Never had an empire of this size been founded so fast. A curious and slightly insane ambition had suddenly swept over these peoples as they tended their flocks in the vast, monotonous expanses of Siberia. They quite suddenly rushed out and seized the world, pursuing a dream equally unlike the cold, methodical greed of the Roman Empire and the religious enthusiasm of the Arabs; this was a dream of universal domination for its own sake, just in order to be able to see other peoples bow down before their flag, to hear them proclaim the glory of the Moghul name and recognize the sovereignty of the great Khan, their mighty chief, over the whole of mankind.

Genghis-Khan and Tamerlane are names which stand out in history as sinister shadows with an aura of blood and fire. There is something incomprehensible about their gigantic and terrifying role in history which makes it seem even more awe-inspiring.

Like almost all primitive forms of worship, the initial religion of the Moghuls was the adoration of the forces of nature. Their main gods were the sun, the earth and the horse. They later adopted most of the beliefs of the peoples who came under their rule, adding one set of beliefs to another.

It is fitting that they should be counted amongst the Moslem invaders of India because at the moment of their entry into India, they had long been in contact with Persians, Turks and Afghans who professed the Islamic faith and had absorbed much of the Arab civilization which at that time dominated all western Asia.

Their extreme religious tolerance and that of the Hindus were a happy coincidence.

Throughout their rule, various attempts were made by both the conquerors and the conquered peoples to merge the many diverse beliefs into a single religion. Nanak, founder of the Sikhs, emperor Akbar himself, and many others all sought to achieve this aim. Yet in spite of all the efforts made, no single religion emerged, and all the many sects continued to live side by side in a spirit of mutual understanding.

It is impossible to say that these invasions gave rise to no new race. The invaders were too few in number to avoid merging quickly with the mass of the vanquished people. In any case, they were themselves of very mixed blood.

True to their spirit of tolerance and conciliation, the Moghuls quickly married into the populations which they found in India. They particularly sought out marriages with the daughters of Rajputs, and soon their facial features, already changed by contact with Afghans and Turks, changed completely. The numerous portraits of Moghuls emperors which have come down to us in the manuscripts usually show features which are longer and more regular than the flat faces, squat noses and thick lips of pure Moghuls.

It is worth nothing that, out of the 700 years of Moslem, rule, the Moghul empire, the only, Moslem power usually mentioned in books, lasted only 200 years.

If we were to retrace the history of Moslem civilization in India, we would have to give a full account of the whole of that Arab civilization. The Moslems of India merely introduced the civilization of the Arabs which

Mosque at Aurengabad. Following pages: small figures with statue of Vishnu; Temple of the Sun at Konarak; a bas-relief from the same temple.

*Left: Vishnu on the fabulous bird Garuda
(Khajurao). Above: Sculpture at Konarak.*

75

had been more or less modified as it crossed Persia, and which then became further altered by mixing, to an extent which varied according to the time and place, with that of the invaded peoples.

The political institutions which the Moslems brought with them were also those of the former Arab kingdoms. They possessed both the qualities which had ensured the prosperity of those kingdoms, and the flaws which had led to their decline. All the Moslem states, in India and elsewhere, were always absolute monarchies, in which the sovereign held in his hands all religious, military and civil power; however, he often delegated this power without supervision to governors who soon tried to make themselves independent of him and found their own kingdoms.

By bringing in Arab civilization, the Moslems introduced into India an enlightened taste for the sciences, letters and the arts. The monuments of their former capitals, Ahmedabad, Gaur, Delhi, Bijapur, etc., prove how enthusiastically they protected the arts. Biographies of the Moslem sovereigns also show us how they gave equal encouragement to both letters and sciences, and how they themselves personally cultivated them, not just in the great cities, but also in fairly minor

Opposite: window, in the ruins of the mosque surrounding the Qtab-Minar, Delhi. Right: a tomb, at Agra. The Taj Mahal, Agra.

76

kingdoms. Early in the 15th century, for example, Firuz Shah, king of the small kingdom of Golconda, managed to cultivate geometry, botany and poetry, and had in his entourage only scholars, poets and historians, while simultaneously fighting a series of wars against the empire of Bijangar.

Since we cannot give the history of the various Moslem civilizations in India, we shall simply present a brief account of the most spectacular of them all, the Moghul civilization.

The Moghul empire in India began in 1526, when Beber took Agra, which was being governed at the time by a prince of the dynasty of Lodi. By the time he died there, he was the sovereign of Hindustan and Kabul. His son Himayun had to fight numerous battles in order to keep his empire intact. Moghul power did not reach its highest point until the 50-year reign of Akbar, the third Moghul emperor, who came to the throne in 1556. This prince, one of the great figures of history, treated Hindus and Moslems alike, and favored marriages between the two peoples, himself setting the example; even if he failed to merge the two religions, he at least did succeed in combining the architectural styles of his subject peoples. He extended his conquests and administered them quite wisely. He had a census taken in his territories and estimates made of the area and quality of the soil in each province, basing the taxes on actual production: only one third of the amount of goods produced went to

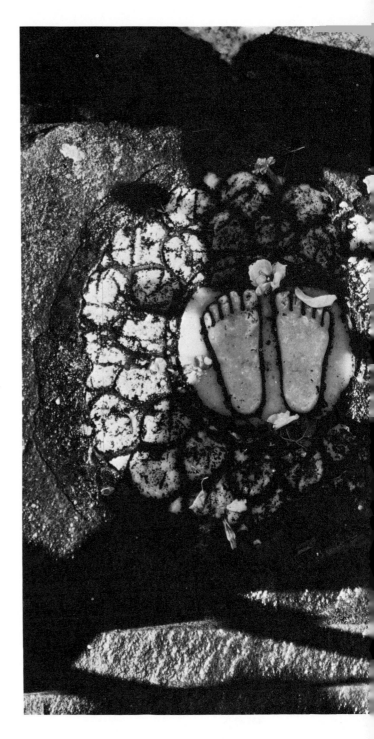

the state and the rest to the farmer. He abolished many taxes, and paid his officers in cash, rather than by assigning territories to them.

The name of the Grand Moghul is still synonymous, in Europe, with absolute power and spectacular displays of wealth; and there are good reasons for such a reputation.

The power of the Moghul emperor was absolute; he exercised it in order to ensure a steady flow of treasure into his court from what was then a very rich country, and then proceeded to spend it in acts of magnificence which have never been surpassed since.

The Moghul emperor spent much of his time in public and, even if the levies he extracted from his subjects were somewhat too frequent, at least he did offer them a virtually non-stop spectacle for them to feast their eyes upon.

In the morning, he appeared on his balcony and gave the crowd a chance to see and acclaim him. This regular morning appearance on the balcony was suspended only if the sovereign was seriously ill. He would come out onto the same balcony again at noon, to watch elephant fights and various military or other exercises which took place in the palace square.

In the afternoon, he held the *durbar,* which was a kind of reception at which the emperor was supposed to listen to anyone who had

Vishnu's "footprint" (tomb of Humayun, Delhi).

anything to say to him. In actual fact, however, it was quite difficult to get anywhere near him: the crowd was separated from the imperial throne by two or three separate levels surrounded by ornate, gilded railings, behind which stood the nobles and brightly-clad guards. But the people seemed satisfied with the mere sight of this magnificent assembly, and the sight, particularly, of the monarch whose face, in the midst of strings of flashing jewels, took on a supernatural air. This spectacle may have helped the people forget the price they were paying for a moment of excitement and enthusiasm which was mingled with a respect bordering on terror.

The need to keep a constant watch on events in all their provinces led the emperors to set up a fast and reliable postal system. The postmen were runners who relayed the messages to each other along the main roads; the edge of the sometimes rather indistinct road was marked by white stones which could be seen at night, so that the runners would not lose their way in the dark.

The state of the roads in the Moghul period seems to have been excellent. Tavernier, who travelled around India in the mid-17th century, claimed that the roads were better maintained in India than in France or Italy. Personal transport took the form of a sedan carried from place to place by agile runners, or a chariot drawn by oxen.

All land within the Moghul empire was regarded as the personal property of the sovereign and was divided into two categories:

land given by the emperor to his army chiefs on condition that it be used for their troops and that an annual payment be made to the treasury; other land was leased to farmers for an annual rent. Like the viceroys, the farmers had absolute power over the people they governed, and, as could be expected, they exacted a frequent and heavy tribute. The peasant, tired of working for someone else, lost interest in his crops and was prepared to till and reap only under duress. Anyone who did succeed in making a little money promptly buried it and went about looking as poor as possible, so as to avoid arbitrary seizure of his savings.

The administration of justice was quite bad; just like the king's ministers, courtiers and wives, the judges were very much swayed in their verdicts by suitable gifts. Admittedly, Akbar did have bells hung up in his palace, so that anyone with an injustice to report could ring them and notify him of their complaint. But in fact, since everyone knew that the use of this procedure would expose them to the wrath of the powerful, it seldom served to remedy any abuses.

The emperor Aurengzeb, who was constantly at war, decided to live permanently in his camp. Drawing heavily on the coffers of his predecessors, he surrounded himself with huge forces, plenty of artillery and a well organized cavalry force. His time was spent in the midst of this formidable yet also magnificent army. His wives, jewels and resplendent wardrobe followed him about on elephants, protected by canon and the dense ranks of his warriors, the whole procession being headed by incense-burners.

Left: tomb of Shah Feraz (in Old Delhi). Right: the Qtab-Minar (230 feet high, Delhi).

Whenever the emperor halted, the tents were erected with astonishing speed. A whole town seemed to spring up out of the earth, complete with well-aligned streets, squares, crossroads and fortifications. Each tent had a special place allotted to it, according to a pre-arranged plan. Mobile palaces provided the monarch with comfort such as was normally found in the most splendid buildings. Aurengzeb's camp had become the true capital of the empire.

Women played a very important role in the court of the Grand Moghuls.

Through their marriages with Hindu princesses, and above all with the daughters of Rajput chiefs, the Moghul emperors—or at least the first few of them—sought to merge this sort, which other Moslems then entered into, following their example.

The Grand Moghuls did not recognize any limit on the number of their wives, this being only one of the areas in which they did not observe the law of Mohammed. Shah Jehan had up to 2,000 women in his harem; yet even these were not enough for him, as he occasionally and quite fearlessly raided the ranks of his emir's wives, looking for mistresses. In this way, he caused great displeasure, as adultery was vehemently disapproved of among Moslems.

While the nobles used to resent any undue imperial attention being paid to their wives, they found such attention flattering when directed towards their daughters. Getting one

of his daughters into the *Mahal,* or imperial harem, was the great ambition of each of these dignitaries. As a concubine, she could be a useful spy; if she succeeded in providing greater satisfaction and became *begum,* or queen, she acquired great influence and the fortune of her family was assured.

The old women who performed a sort of supervisory function in the harem were often powerful enough to command the respect of viceroys and even of foreign kings. Like anyone else who enjoyed the slightest power within the empire, they were thoroughly venal and ready to sell their patronage to the highest bidder.

The magnificence to be found inside the harem was quite prodigious. Each woman had her slaves and her dancing girls and put on entirely new clothes and new jewelry each day.

Some of them, the *begums*—a word meaning "free from all care"—were fed by the emperor's cooks; the others, the concubines, had to draw on the gifts they received for their maintenance. Shah Jehan built the superb Taj Mahal as a mausoleum for the one woman among his many wives whom he loved most and whose death upset him most severely. This uniquely wonderful monument is one of the world's most beautiful buildings.

The Moghuls, like the other Moslems before them, always had a strong attachment to literature, science and the arts. Artists, scholars and poets, whatever their origin, were always welcome at their courts. The monuments left by the Moghuls, which could

rival anything in the West, are still a source of admiration today. The sciences were also highly cultivated under the Moghuls: they founded schools of astronomy and observatories. Their interest dated back several centuries; for example, in 1259, the khan of the Moghuls, Hulagu, had brought to his court the most distinguished Arab scholars and built a great observatory at Megarah. When Tamerlane established the seat of his gigantic empire in Samarkand, he also surrounded himself with scholars; in the mid-fifteenth century, his grandson Olug-Beg built a huge observatory equipped with magnificent instruments, including a guadrant said to be as tall as Hagia Sophia, and with which he himself made some very precise astronomical observations. He published these in an important work which deals with major questions of astronomy and gives very accurate positions for certain stars.

The Grand Moghuls were not merely patrons of the arts and sciences; as we have seen, several of them were themselves accomplished men of letters and scientists. Many had a passion for literature, particularly for poetry, which resulted in the writing of some remarkable books. The celebrated Tamerlane, who was reported to have built a pyramid at Baghdad using a hundred thousand human heads, founded schools, cultivated the sciences and wrote a number of important books, passing his intellectual tastes on to his descendants Baber, Jehangir, etc. Baber's *Memoirs,* which have rightly

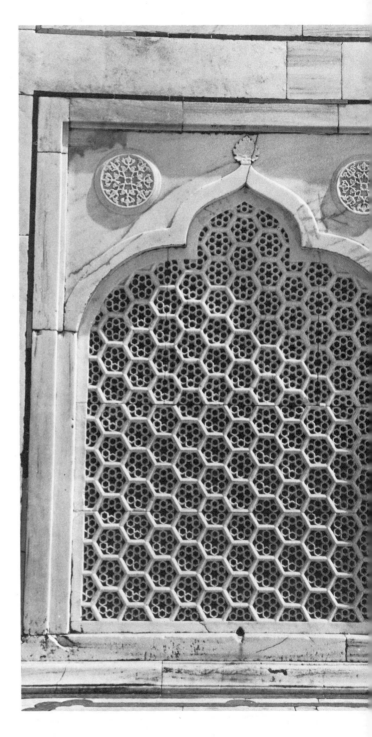

been compared to Caesar's Commentaries, may be regarded as among the finest manifestations of this literary form. They tell us more about that special blend of savagery and civilization which underlies the Moghul character than we can learn from all the writings of the historians.

The bold Baber, who was also a renowned wit and scholar, was one of the most powerful conquerors the world has ever known; he embodies the adventurous, the sophisticated and the barbarous qualities of his race. Already head of a village when only twelve years old, he died at the age of 50 as emperor of India, which he had conquered with 12,000 men.

Left and above: bust of a woman (16th century). Following pages: ornamental couples from various parts of the Temple of the Sun, Konarak.

Divine couple (Khajurao).   Right: another couple (National Museum, Delhi).

Left, above and below: Lovers, from a) Konarak, b) Patna, and c) Khajurao.

6. The Literature of India

India has produced an abundance of literature, most of which has come down to us. Barely two centuries ago, when the study of Sanskrit enabled a number of Europeans to lift the veil covering a hitherto unknown literature, it was thought that a whole world of new and marvellous things was certain to emerge from this obscure, mysterious past. A commonly held belief was that the source of all human civilization and religion had been discovered, and that by going back to the true sources of our race, it would prove possible to recover the lost golden age and the secrets of man's destiny.

This enthusiasm quickly susbsided. It was seen that, however interesting the lives and ideas of the ancients peoples of India might have been, they had no solutions to offer for any of the major problems which they, like us, had tackled. The ultimate word of wisdom, capable of satisfying our souls permanently was clearly not going to come from the banks of the Ganges.

Moreover, their importance from the purely literary point of view had also been vastly overrated. Critics had gallantly ranked them above the masterpieces of Greek and Roman literature. Yet several of the qualities which we admire in the writings of classical antiquity tend to make a reading of the Hindu books fairly painful. The sense of order, the

Civa, king of the dance (13th century).

clarity, the proportions, harmony and sobriety which strike us as so elegant and perfect in the works of Greek and Roman poets and prose writers have made us hard to please; our modern skepticism has heightened our distaste for the exaggerated and the marvellous. Readers formed in this way are unlikely to find much to admire in the vast, rambling, endless works of Hindu antiquity, with their heavy emphasis on the supernatural.

However, one does sometimes come across refreshingly simple statements of human feelings and pictures of the soul or of nature, which seem all the more marvellous in the midst of such wild excesses of the imagination and such prodigious exaggerations.

We have already spoken of the Vedic hymns. Of course, Vedic literature does not consist solely of the Rig Veda: there are also hymns, maxims and treatises (Sutras).

The Vedic books, which were begun a thousand years before Christ, must have been revised many times before they were put into definitive shape in writing. They could be compared to a kind of collective encyclopedia, revised and completed, by the editors at each new edition, with the help of new contributors.

The thousand or so prayers contained in the Rig Veda are the most interesting parts of the Vedas, from the literary point of view. Roughly one half are devoted to Indra, god of the sky, and to Agni, god of fire, the other half being devoted to a great variety of divinities: the sun, nature, the clouds, etc.

Left: the "general of the apes", from the Ramayana. Right: frieze devoted to the dance.

The gigantic epic of Mahabharata is one of the longest works of ancient India, and perhaps of all time. It runs to 215,000 lines, whereas the Iliad had only 15,000 lines, the Odyssey 12,000 and the Aeneid 10,000. It is the equivalent of 15 normal-size tomes each of 500 pages.

The Mahabharata consists of an original core, to which successive additions were made later. This huge epic took centuries to write and was certainly not the work of one man; at least a thousand years elapsed between the composition of the original text and the final changes made in it. So its exact age is difficult to determine; it is unlikely, however, that the most modern parts date from after the third century A.D.

The Mahabharata is of central importance to the Hindus; it is as sacred to them as the Bible is to Christians and Jews and the Koran to Moslems.

The title Mahabharata, or Great Bharata, is an abbreviation for "great history of the Bharata race". It tells the story of the struggle between the Pandavas and the Kuravas, ancient branches of the lunar dynasty of the Bharatides, whose seat was in the ancient city of Hastinapura, near Delhi.

The poem begins with invocations, pro-

logues and genealogies, and continues with a rambling narrative full of digressions and repetitions which make this book very heavy going for a European. Sub-plots and legends are loosely mixed in a way which suggests that the authors made no attempt to fit together all the parts of this mosaic.

This endless epic has rightly been described as artistocratic and sacerdotal in nature, since the characters moving through it are exclusively gods, priests and kings. The common people, craftsmen and tradesmen are not even mentioned. However, there are some remarkable passages in this very long work which stand comparison with the finest passages of Homer. Its moral content is high—certainly higher than that of the Iliad and the Odyssey; but many European readers do not readily find it interesting because of its numerous, visible flaws.

The Ramayana is of only slightly less importance than the Mahabharata; the Vedas and these two epics are the three major works of Sanskrit literature.

Though it also dates from several centuries before Christ, the Ramayana is a little more recent than the Mahabharata, and has correspondingly fewer interpolated passages. It is only 48,000 lines long, that is, a quarter of the length of the earlier epic. According to Hindu tradition, it was written by the god Vishnu.

The Ramayana is the story of the battles fought by Rama to win back the beautiful Sita, his wife, who has been kidnapped by the demon Ravana, king of the Rakshasas, the evil spirits which lived on the island of Lanka (Ceylon).

Like one of the heroes of the Mahabharata, Rama is a god made man, an incarnation of Vishnu. Monkeys and vultures fight on his side in battle. Again, as in the Mahabharata, events take place in a world of fantasy. The general meaning of the poem seems to be a struggle between the principles of good and evil.

The stories told are slightly entangled, yet on the whole are quite interesting, and the

numerous maxims on each page are often extremely curious.

It is certain that this collection of works was written in very early Antiquity; some scholars believe that a number of the fables it contains were imitated by Aesop; but the Sanskrit works of which they form a part clearly date from several periods, as shown, for example, by the reference to an astronomer who lived in about the 6th century A.D.

By the first half of the 6th century A.D., the fame of the Indian fables had spread as far as Persia; Khosru Nurshivan, of the Sassanid dynasty, who reigned between 531 and 579, sent a learned doctor to translate the Panchatantra into the Pehelvi language. The successors of the Persian king kept the precious book until the Arabs destroyed their empire in 652. A century later, the Khalif Abassid Almansur happened to find a copy which had somehow escaped the destruction of the Persian library, and had it translated into Arabic.

As the centuries went by, the popularity of these fables steadily grew. In the 10th century, the Panchatantra was translated into Persian verse, and, on the orders of Suleiman, a Turkish version was produced, also in the 10th century. It was also translated into Greek towards the end of the 11th century; into Hebrew in the 13th, and German in the 14th. Early in the 14th century, Raymond de Béziers translated it into Latin from a Spanish text which he himself had translated from the Arabic, for Queen Joan of Navarre, wife of Philip-the-Fair. There is no major language into which this immortal work has not been more or less faithfully translated. It figured prominently in the literature of the Middle Ages; indeed, most of the European fables and legends—including the fables of La Fontaine—are derived from it.

The Hipotadesa, a closely related work, is quite as famous, though much more modern. It is really little more than a new edition of the Panchatantra, abridged in some parts and expanded in others by the addition of new fables taken from an unknown anthology, doubtless dating from early antiquity.

The Hipotadesa has also been translated into most languages.

Many Hindu tales are known in Europe through the "Thousand and One Nights". Although most of the stories in this collection are of Arabic origin, it does contain several Hindu tales; but they have been so extensively refashioned that it is often difficult to tell that they originated in India.

Hindu plays are partly written in prose and partly in verse: the language used varies according to the person speaking. The higher castes usually speak Sanskrit, and the lower speak Prakrit.

Although these plays sometimes use quite licentious dialogue, they are without any doubt morally superior to our modern drama. Adultery, which is so often the standard fare of our theatre, is the exception in Hindu drama. Love admittedly plays a big part in them, but it is love followed by marriage. The social rules strictly prohibited the coveting of other people's wives. It is true that the role of the courtesan is quite as prominent as it is modern drama; but, as we have explained, these courtesans enjoyed a more elevated status in the Hindu society of that time, rather like the situation of the *hetaira* in the Greek world; they were cultivated and well-educated women who enjoyed an esteem which is not accorded to their counterparts in modern society.

Hindu drama is almost always of the fairy-tale variety, involving exclusively supernatural events, constant apparitions by gods, marriages between goddesses and ordinary mortals. When a situation becomes too complicated, the gods are called in to provide a dénouement.

Among the many Hindu plays known in Europe, we shall mention only those by Kalidasa, who was assumed to have lived in about the 6th century AD. Of all his works (The Cloud Messenger, The Origin of the Young God, Ourvaci loved by a hero, etc.) Shakuntala is the most famous, and has been translated into about a dozen languages.

It was much admired by Goethe, Lamartine and other writers of the period when the discovery of Sanskrit literature was still thought to have opened up and entirely new horizon for man. Although it falls far short of meriting the enthusiastic praise heaped upon it when it first came to light, this is nevertheless an example of a play in which the qualities of Hindu writers most clearly offset their defects.

With the exception of history, which is a genre for which the Hindus showed no aptitude at all—so much so that one can safely say that they have not a single book on the subject to their credit—there is hardly a subject on which they did not write. Numerous books were written on philosophy, religion, legislation, etc.; a number of treatises were written on the sciences, but these are of a pretty low standard.

There is no room here for us to give even a simple list of all these works; so we shall mention only the Puranas, because of the importance attached to them by the Hindus.

The word Purana (meaning "ancient") is the term used to refer to the religious books of various ages, which have been rightly described as a depositary for popular mythology. They also give the legendary history of the main early dynasties of India. This work totals more than 800,000 lines of verse, amounting in fact to 18 authentic encyclopedias, which make absolutely indigestible reading.

Besides those mentioned in this chaper, the only Hindu books of any interest to us here are the philosophical works contained in the Upanishads. Their philosophical daring remains unequalled to this day; indeed, one has to admit that, 2,000 years ago, India had begun pondering on the great issues which have been raised in the West only in within the last century, and that, in doing so, it did not shrink from the most drastic solutions.

A tower at the temple of Sri Meenakshi, Madurai.

7. The Monuments of India

An archeologist visiting India without any knowledge of the country's past other than the fact that it had contained several powerful civilizations would be astonished at what he would find there, and perhaps even more astonished at what he would find missing. Not a single trace is left of the oldest civilization of all, which began more than 15 centuries before Christ, and the power of which is extolled in literary works. As for the civilization which followed it after more than a thousand years of preparation, he would find traces which, while giving some idea of its greatness, would not suffice to explain its history. When the monuments do appear, quite abruptly, just three centuries before Christ, they are of such high quality that even the monuments of much later ages scarcely seem to equal them.

Nowhere in India does the observer find those periods of gestation or preparation, which the remnants of other civilizations almost always reveal. In some regions, he will find that monuments appear suddenly at one point in history, increase in number for two or three centuries, and then abruptly disappear. Their appearance in history was preceded and, also followed, by the most total obscurity. Elsewhere, he might discover clear evidence of Greek or Persian influences, but these also are confined to certain limited areas and come to an abrupt end.

With the exception of certain caves, which cannot properly be called architecture, the oldest monuments of India date from barely three centuries before Christ. However, we have definite proof that before that time the Hindus had an architecture of their own, and that they built towns and palaces. We know this not only from the descriptions contained in the ancient epics of the Mahabharata and the Ramayana, but also from the degree of perfection attained by those of the older monuments which have survived—the bas-reliefs on the balustrade at Bharhut, for example—since such high standards can only be the result of a long artistic past. It is assumed that all these buildings have been lost, because they were made of wood and bricks, only their foundations being made of stone.

For this reason, India must have begun to acquire these stone monuments, some of which have come down to us, roughly about the time of king Ashoka, in the third century B.C. A number of authors believe that their builders started by imitating the older wooden structures.

The oldest and the richest monuments of India are the temples and monasteries which were hewn out of the sides of mountains.

With the exception of a number of underground chambers in Bihar, dating from the 5th century B.C., which are little more than excavations, the oldest such monuments are as late as the 2nd century B.C. They continue until the 8th century A.D., that is, for about a thousand years. When Buddhism disappeared from India, they also disappeared almost completely. Nine tenths of these monuments

are, in fact, Buddhist, only one tenth being Brahman or Jainist.

These cave-buildings, hewn out of the rock, consisted of temples and monasteries, of which approximately 30 and 1,000, respectively, have been recorded.

Some of them are fairly unadorned excavations; but many of them, including some of the oldest ones, are decorated with an abundance of sculptures and finely chiselled work which is without parallel in other civilizations.

Full view of the underground temples at Ajunta. Right: mural sculptures in temple no. 9.

The most remarkable of these temples are the ones at Bhaja, Karli, Ellora, Badami, Ajanta, etc. A brief account of the temples at Ajanta will suffice to give some idea of the way they were built and the formidable amount of work which must have gone into them.

Left: peristyle of temple no. 8, and, above, inside view of temple no. 24, at Ajanta.

The Ajanta temples are dug out of the side of a steep rock face looking down into a forbidding ravine and the swirling waters of a mountain torrent, 55 miles from Aurengabad. One has to climb over heaps of rock in order to get to it. The mere sight of this grim, inaccessible spot is ample evidence that the monks who took refuge therein must have really valued solitude and sought to keep people away from their retreat by all possible means. If the small number of Europeans who venture up to Ajanta from nearby Bombay is any indication, their wishes have been amply fulfilled.

The varied age of these temples proves that, for many centuries, generations of men lived in their dark vaults. The immense amount of work required to carve out the whole the inside of the mountain is unimaginable unless one thinks of the many centuries it must have taken.

The oldest buildings at Ajanta probably date from about 150 years before Christ, while the most recent are from the 7th century A.D. Abundance of ornament rather than artistic quality is the main difference between them. As is the case elsewhere in India, the quality of the monuments follows no chronological pattern.

The more recent temples at Ajanta are characterized above all by the reproductions of the figure of Buddha, which are repeated almost endlessly. The *dagobas,* or altars, are covered with sculptures, including some showing Buddha after he had attained the state of beatitude.

In front of most of the underground temples and monasteries at Ajanta there is a stone balcony supported by pillars which, like the monument itself, are hewn out of the rock.

Several of the temples at Ajanta have monasteries attached to them, usually as a separate structure. They consist of cells arranged around an inner hall and each containing a stone bed. The central hall, which is often quite vast, was used as a temple, and even contains a number of side-chapels devoted to individual saints, as in the Catholic churches. The last of these monasteries grew so big that extra pillars

Temple no. 19, at Ajanta.

*Left and above: figures carved on transverse
beams, in a temple at Ajanta.*

had to be built to hold up the ceiling of the temple around which the cells were arranged, even though this ceiling consisted simply of the upper part of the excavation in the mountainside. Ajanta has underground chambers 100 feet long and supported by 24 massive pillars, which are only slightly more than 13 feet tall.

At the end of these great underground halls there is usually a colossal statue of Buddha surrounded by various figures. Both pillars and ceiling are covered with colored sculptures and arabesques. The walls are covered with painted frescoes depicting scenes from the life of Buddha. Even though they are in very poor condition, these frescoes are of great interest, as they are the only paintings

Above: decoration on a door in temple no. 26, at Ajanta. Right: sculpture, Sarnath.

which have come down to us from ancient India. They probably date from the 5th century A.D. The striking features, the dress and the hairstyles of the persons depicted in them are those of quite a different race from that which can be seen in the earliest monuments of Bhaja, Karli, Bharhut, Sanchi, etc.

The effect produced by these underground temples is surpassed only by the sight of the temples at Ellora, with the colossal statue of Buddha, seemingly surrounded by giants, just visible by torchlight between the massive

112

stone columns at the end of huge underground chambers.

Stupas or topes look rather like European burial mounds. They are usually hemispherical, as at Sanchi, but occasionally take the form of a tower, as at Sarnath. They are surrounded by a sort of stone balustrade, covered with sculptures. Monumental doors stand at the entrance.

The great tope at Sanchi will give an adequate idea of this kind of structure. It is one of the most ancient and most beautiful monuments in India. The tope itself dates from before 250 B.C., during the reign of Ashoka. The balustrade and the doors are from the 1st century A.D. Apart from temples built into rock, India has very few monuments from that period; those at Sanchi probably owe their survival to their remote location. When we consider that other monuments of the same period, for example those at Bharhut, were just as splendidly adorned as these, it becomes clear that the architecture of the major cities must have reached an impressive degree of refinement.

The tope at Sanchi, and other similar structures, were built to mark some sacred spot, or to commemorate some religious event.

Great Buddhist temples above ground are extremely rare, not because few of them were built, but doubtless because they were built of materials, particularly of brick, which could not withstand the harsh Indian climate. The only one which escaped destruction,

Ajanta. Opposite: sculptures from temple no. 20. Below: frieze between vault and capitals, temple no. 26.

and this was due exclusively to restoration work carried out from time to time, is the Buddh-Gaya temple, which was built 100 years before Christ at the place in which Buddha was standing when, according to the legend, he achieved supreme wisdom.

For the 800 million human beings who still profess Buddhism, which means for most of the peoples of Asia, the three holiest places in the world are: Kapilavastu, where Buddha was born; Benares, where he first preached his doctrine; and Buddh-Gaya, where he achieved supreme wisdom. No-one knows for certain where exactly the first of these three towns was; but the second two are still in existence, and are among the main centers of pilgrimage in India.

The Buddh-Gaya temple is in the form of a pyramid with a square base, nine stories high, resting on a cube about 26 feet high, with sides of 49 feet. The total height of the building is 170 feet. Inside, there are three small sanctuaries, one on top of the other.

Excavations around Buddh-Gaya have unearthed large quantities of sculptures, pillars, votive stupas, etc., most of which are very old. They now stand in the garden surrounding the temple.

In spite of the powerful barriers which have always tended to isolate India from the rest of the world, it has nevertheless been invaded, ever since early antiquity, by the most diverse peoples. The conquerors—Aryans, Moghuls, Persians, Afghans—all came across the Himalayas, most of them taking the pass from Afghanistan. In the 5th century B.C., the Persians invaded under Darius; they were followed by the Greeks under Alexander in 330 B.C.: later, the Arabs and the Moghuls, conquered the whole peninsula. India has therefore been exposed to many foreign influences and has been in contact with many foreign peoples.

Obviously, then, we must expect to find in the architecture of India a reflection of these foreign influences; yet, with the exception of Moslem influences, they are not readily perceptible. Until it came under the law of Islam, India had always absorbed its various conquerors, without allowing itself to be influenced by them, and in this is somewhat like ancient Egypt. Though twenty different peoples, including Greeks and Romans, had invaded the land of the Pharaohs, it somehow managed to preserve its religion, language, architecture and social structure. Only the Moslem civilization was strong enough to entirely change its religion, language and arts.

The earliest foreign artistic influences appeared in India on the banks of the Indus. It was here that relations were established first with the Persians and then with the

At Konarak: one of the wheels of the temple of the Sun. It is ten feet across.

Greeks. The writings of Herodotus, confirmed by cuneiform inscriptions, prove that, 400 years before Christ, the kingdoms along the banks of the Indus were paying tribute to the king of the Persians.

Persian influence on certain architectural motifs can be detected in various fragments of monuments, the oldest of which date from only a few years before the birth of Christ; it is particularly apparent in columns which have bell-shaped capitals, with animals lying back to back on top; the prototype of this style can be found in the palace of the Achaemenid kings at Persepolis. Columns of this sort may be seen in many ancient temples in India, especially at Nassik, Sanchi, etc., but above all in the region near Peshawar. The oldest ones of all are at Bharhut; these date from 250 B.C.

These Persian influences were later replaced by Greek influences, these latter occurring only in the valleys of Kabul and Kashmir; they are most notable in statues and columns. The columns are Doric in Kashmir, Ionic in Taxila, and Corinthian in the valley of Kabul. They show traces, moreover, of Buddhist beliefs, particularly in the form of the statue of Buddha surrounded by acanthus leaves.

The monuments of the Orissa coast are among the oldest and the most remarkable in India. They were built between the 5th and

Konarak. Above, the temple of the Dance, seen from the temple of the Sun.

8th centuries A.D. The underground temples which can be seen in the same area are much older, but their architecture is not related to that of the temples which we are about to describe.

Although the temples of the province of Orissa were built over a span of seven to eight centuries, the main features of their style are quite uniform. It differs greatly from the style of the temples of southern India, lacking both towers with superimposed floors and rooms supported on columns.

On the outside, the temples at Orissa are shaped like pyramids, but, instead of having straight sides, like the temples of southern India, they have curved sides.

The top of these pyramids is flat, ending in a sort of ribbed crown, rather like a flattened melon. They are covered with ornaments and sculptures.

A porch, also covered with a pyramid-shaped tower, stands in front of the building. After the porch, and in the same axis, there are often one or two rooms, one serving as a dancing room and the other as a refectory.

The whole building is surrounded by a wall, along which there are several ornate doors with square-sided pyramid roofs over them.

The main façade of the temple always faces east, so that the divinity in the sanctuary will always be looking towards the rising sun.

The proportions and dimensions of the temple and each of its parts are closely governed by a set of strict rules. The only area in which artists could give free rein to their fantasy was in ornamental detail and in the sculptures.

The walls of the temple are enormously thick—far thicker than the stability of the building requires. This was because the ancient Hindu books on architecture stipulated that the walls of a building should be equivalent to four tenths of its total space, leaving only six tenths usable space inside. Besides giving the monument a majestic look, this huge volume of material also has the effect of making it virtually indestructible. In a country which has earthquakes and a great variety of bad weather, this use of apparently excessive amounts of building materials might not, in actual fact, be as pointless as theory suggests.

Instead of being built partly or wholly out of bricks, as is the case in southern India, the Orissa temples are built exclusively out of stone, usually sandstone. The stone sections were hewn and fitted together so perfectly that no cement was needed to hold them in place. Sometimes, iron clamps were used to strengthen edges which stuck out too much. The architraves, instead of being made of stone, were occasionally replaced by wrought iron beams.

Like many ancient temples in India, the temples of Mount Abu, which we shall describe next, are located in a rather inaccessible place; indeed, it seems that the builders of temples went out of their way to make it

Fantastic animal, at the entrance to the "fort" at Gwalior.

as hard as possible for people to reach their temples. These temples stand at the top of a deserted mountain, at an altitude of 5,600 feet. They are built entirely of white marble, a material which is not found at all in that region; the blocks of marble had therefore to be hoisted to the top of the mountain, a feat of transport which must have required gigantic efforts. An even harder task was involved in the cutting of these masses of marble into the necessary pieces. Yet the artistic result was certainly worth the energy expended. Europe has not one monument of the Gothic period which can equal the fine stonework of Mount Abu.

The outside of the temples on Mount Abu, however, is completely devoid of ornaments and sculptures; there is no indication of the marvels that lie within.

This region boasts many other splendid monuments also: the palace of Gwalior, for example, built about 1500. It is 330 feet long and 100 feet high. Its main façade, the one covered entirely with enamelled bricks, faces east: it covers two floors and consists of a massive rectangle cut at equal intervals by six round towers with cupolas. The enamelled tiles covering part of its walls create a magnificent overall effect; though the designs on these tiles are Hindu in origin, the craftsmanship involved is clearly of Persian origin.

Inside the palace are two sets of small chambers arranged around small courtyards. The biggest of these exquisitely designed

121

chambers is only 33 feet by 20 feet.

The architecture of Gujarat, and particularly that of Ahmedabad, which may be regarded as a good example of it, has a combination of Moslem and Jaina elements which distinguish it from the styles we have been describing.

Founded in the 11th century A.D., Ahmedabad was, for a hundred and fifty years the capital of a province the size of Great Britain. Notwithstanding the great diversity of the races inhabiting the region, its population has always been remarkably autonomous. The city itself has always had a reputation for hard work; throughout history, it has been a lively center for the arts and the sciences. The region was known in very early times, as much trade with Arabia and Egypt was transacted there.

The most important monuments of this province are attributable to the disciples of Jainism, which was a religious sect similar to Buddhims, practiced mainly in Gujarat. The Mohammedans merely adapted them to their own forms of worship.

The city owes its name to the sultan Ahmed, grandson of Muzzafar, who moved his capital there in 1412, and gave it his name.

The earlier Hindu monuments built in the Jaina style were simply converted into mosques, while those built later kept to the same style; were it not for the addition of arcades, minarets and Arabic inscriptions, the monuments of Ahmedabad could be regarded as purely Hindu.

Jaina temple of Parsvanatha, at Khajurao.

In 1572, Ahmedabad was conquered by the emperor Akbar, and thenceforth became part of the Moghul empire; for 150 years it was governed by viceroys sent from Delhi, including Shah Jehan and Aurengzeb, who were later to become emperors.

During the period of Moghul domination, Ahmedabad attained the peak of its splendor, with a reputation as the most beautiful city in India, and perhaps even in the world. It had a population of over two million; its travellers and traders were in constant touch with Arabia, Africa and the whole of the rest of India. It was famous for the excellence of the brocade, velvet, silk, satin and paper which it manufactured. The fine work done by its craftsmen in wood, gold and ivory would be difficult to surpass. It is in Gujarat that the boxes of inlaid sandalwood known as Bombay boxes are made.

The architecture of Gujarat, most fully represented by Ahmedabad, offers a striking example of the variations of Moslem architecture which may be seen in the different parts of India. Owing to the predominance of Hindu elements, the monuments of Ahmedabad have a special quality about them which can be found in no other region. The addition of arcades, minarets and Arabic inscriptions gives them a Moslem appearance, whereas their ornaments place them squarely within the Jaina style, the most striking examples of which are to be found at Mount Abu.

The Ahmedabad mosques were designed in the same way as all Moslem mosques; a huge rectangular courtyard surrounded by covered galleries. On one of the sides of the rectangle, the gallery is deeper and is used as a sanctuary; this side is covered with three ample domes, supported, as all domes in the Jaina style are, by twelve columns.

The monuments of the region which we are about to consider are among the most interesting in India. Several of them, the temple of Ambernath, for example, are not significantly different from the monuments which we have studied from other regions, whereas others, such as the ones at Ellora, have an architecture all of their own.

The centre of India also has underground temples which, instead of being exclusively Buddhist, like those at Karli, Ajanta, etc., are devoted either solely to the cult of Brahmanism, like the temples at Elephanta, or to both Brahmanism and Buddhism, like those at Ellora.

The underground excavations which make up the temples of Elora are about thirty in number; they are to be found running a total length of over a mile in the west side of the mountain. The entrance to them is now barely visible under ancient trees and jungle undergrowth, in a deep ravine. These temples and monasteries, in which so many generations of men used to live, and which remind one strongly of the most colossal monuments

Above and right: bas-reliefs, at Elephanta.

Above: first chamber of the under-ground temple at Elephanta. Right: view of temple no. 16 at Ellora.

Above: courtyard of temple no. 16 at Ellora.
Left: columns of temple no. 1, at Elephanta.

Chamber in temple no. 15 at Ellora: in the center, statue of sacred cow. Right: Interior of temple no. 2 at Ellora.

of ancient Egypt, are now silent; the only movement to be seen amongst their majestic grandeur is that of the groups of visitors who have come to admire them, and an occasional beggar or two.

The various temples of Ellora were built at different times. The oldest one, the temple of Viswakarma, dates from 500 A.D., while the most recent, the Kailasa, was built not later than 800 A.D.

A whole volume could easily be devoted to an enumeration and description of all the temples at Ellora. The most outstanding of them are the temple of Indra and the Kailasa. This latter one is not entirely underground, as its main section is a monument standing apart from the mountain; yet it is surrounded by numerous excavations which are related to it, and which extend quite some distance into the mountain.

The Kailasa, dedicated to Shiva, is one of the monuments on which the Hindu artists really gave free rein to their fantasy; the sculptures which it contains present the whole Hindu pantheon, as well as the episodes of the great epic, the Mahabharata.

The temple stands in a rectangular court-yard, the sides of which are the rock faces of the mountain. A number of chambers, decorated with sculptures, have been dug into these walls.

The temple is a single block, 100 feet high. A gateway adorned with pilasters provides access to the courtyard. The interior consists of a huge hall supported by pillars and pilasters, and surrounded by chapels. The whole building is surrounded by lions, elephants and assorted fantastic animals which seem to be supporting it.

Near the temple are two obelisks; there are also two huge elephants hewn out of a single block of stone.

The temple of Karnak, at Luxor, in Egypt, is certainly a splendid monument; but whereas Karnak seems to be the work of a people of giants, Kailasa and the temple of Indra at Ellora seem to be the work of a people of wizards. Even Aladdin, with his magic lamp, could hardly have dreamt up anything so fantastic. Unfortunately, photographs give only a partial idea of what it looks like; one really has to try to imagine a huge, fantastic cathedral, hewn out of a single block of stone, artificially separated from a mountain. On the sides of the cliff, which had to be created in order to isolate this gigantic block, the hands of artists from a world quite different from our own have dug a series of temples which disappear into the side of the mountain. All of these stuctures are covered with statues of gods, goddesses, monsters and animals in poses which only a delirious imagination could have contrived. Terrifying divinities, guarded by stone giants who seem to glare down threateningly at any visitor rash enough to venture too close;

132

snarling monsters; smiling goddesses, stretching out their arms tenderly; dancing girls in lascivious positions; gods and goddesses locked in a furious amorous embrace: such is the spectacle the visitor sees at Ellora. There is an endless procession of idols which seem as old as time, of supernatural beings, of dancing-girls and sirens. Whichever way you turn, and wherever you point your flashlight, you will see their shadowy forms looking back at you, smilingly or menacingly. The total effect is almost hallucinatory, as if one had been transported into a magic world. Certainly, a huge distance separates the stiff, cold statues of our Gothic cathedrals from these lively, pulsating stone shapes, which are so real that the people represented in them look as if they are about to step down and start walking about.

The pagodas of the south of India show some noteworthy differences of craftsmanship, but they all seem to have been built according to the same plan, and clearly belong to the same family.

The various structures which make up a great pagoda are always surrounded by a rectangular wall, sometimes by several concentric rectangular walls, each of which usually has a door, in the shape of a flattened pyramid standing on a parallelepiped, on its four sides. This door, or *gopura,* is covered with statues, and sometimes reaches a height of 195 feet. These pyramid-shaped doors are what give the pagodas of southern

Sacred cow in the middle of temple no. 15 at Ellora (see page 131).

India their characteristic appearance. Their size entitles each of them to be regarded as a real temple.

The pagodas of the towns of Bijanagar, Madurai and Sriningam are some of the more curious monuments in the south of India, the last of them being over half a mile long, and therefore probably the biggest temple in the world. Bijanagar contains ruins of all sorts. For many years the capital of the south, this city must also have been one of the biggest cities in the world, judging by its ruins. Now it is deserted, except for some wild animals.

The large number of Moslem kingdoms in India during different periods led to great variations of style from one province to another. The conquerors themselves belonged to different races, and the provinces which they invaded already had their own architectural styles. When one studies the monuments of Ahmedabad, Delhi, Lahore, Bijapur, etc., one senses immediately the wide differences in the origins of these buildings, though Hindu influence is fairly pervasive. The Moslems of India, unlike those of Egypt and Spain, never succeeded in creating entirely original monuments, such as the Kait Bey mosque in Cairo, or the Alhambra in Grenada, for example.

The oldest Moslem momuments, such as the Koutab in Delhi and the great mosque of Ajmir, date from the end of the 12th century; the last important monuments they built

Left: view of the temples at Madurai.

date from 500 years later, at the end of the 17th century.

English writers often use to term *pathan* to designate the Moslem style found in India before the Moghul period, from the name of the dynasty reigning at the time.

Although monuments in the Moghul style account for a small proportion of Moslem monuments, they are nonetheless virtually the only ones widely known in Europe. This is, after all, readily explicable, since the main ones are situated in the two famous cities which Europeans have most often visited: Lahore and Delhi; it is also true that they create a powerful visual effect, yet, from the artistic point of view, they are definitely not without their rivals.

The style which the Moghuls brought with them into India was, like their religion, of Arabic origin; and, like it, this style was

Photo taken at Kanchipuram.

changed as it had crossed Persia. A whole century before Baber, Tamerlane builts monuments in Samarkand in which Persian influence predominated. It is this Persian influence which accounts for the bulbous domes peculiar to the Moghuls, walls covered with enamelled tiles, which are so common in Lahore, the pointed shape of the arcades, and the gigantic doors crowned with a half-dome.

The State of Nepal is bounded by parallel Himalayan ranges which separate India from Tibet. Thanks to its isolation, and independence, it has proved able to keep certain ancient customs intact. Its architecture is exceedingly interesting. Many monuments show a clear combination of Hindu and Chinese elements; yet in others the two styles have been merged so closely and so subtly that the observer is convinced he is seeing an entirely new style.

Islamic designs: a) Banqueting-hall in Delhi; b) Taj Mahal mosque. Right: courtyard wall, Agra.

136

8. The Sciences and the Arts

The Hindus got all their scientific knowledge from the peoples with which they have come into contact, and made very little scientific progress of their own. A study of the state of the Hindu's scientific knowledge at any given point in history, therefore, would simply be tantamount to writing a scientific history of these other peoples.

The mental make-up of the Hindus readily explains why they have made no serious progress with the scientific knowledge which has reached them from foreign sources. The Hindu mind, which is so subtle in philosophy and so ingenious in the arts, lacks the qualities of judgment and the precise habits of mind which are necessary for a serious study of science. In any kind of scientific knowledge, they have always performed poorly; they quickly assimilate the results obtained by others, but are unable to take them much further.

The two peoples from whom the Hindus seem to have borrowed all of their scientific knowledge are the Greeks and the Arabs.

Their poor showing in the theoretical sciences did not prevent the Hindus from achieving some quite advanced practical knowledge, as witnessed by the state of their early architecture and their industrial arts. They knew all about glass, paint, distillation, the art of extracting metals, of making steel and preparing certain metallic salts. But this practical knowledge, the product of experience, apart from the fact that much of it must have been imported anyway, remained for them unconnected with any theory or general principles.

For thousands of years, India was the richest country in the world, a country in which the arts constantly flourished, regardless of the various political upheavals which occurred from time to time. Ever since the beginning of recorded time, the peoples of the world have prized its artworks, its jewelry and its fabrics; for thousands of years, in a sense, India drained off vast amounts of money from the rest of the world. Dynasties came and went, revolutions took place and fortunes consequently changed hands, but those fortunes always stayed within the peninsula and were used by those who owned them, as they had been used by their predecessors before them, to build temples and palaces, and to do all in their power to encourage the arts of India, one of the country's finest resources.

Hindu ornamentation is distinguished by its lavish exaggerations and an immense abundance of detail, both of these being precisely the dominant traits of the Hindu people, as can be seen from their literary, religious and philosophical works.

No other people has made such an extensive use of statues for ornamental purpose. Their temples, and particularly their sanctuaries, are covered with thousands of statues and bas-reliefs; curiously, however, documents dealing with statues are almost completely missing from books on the Hindu arts.

Anatomical accuracy is sometimes neglected in Hindu statues, giving way to the

Torso of Buddha (Mathura).

Princess with lady-in-waiting, fresco (at Ajanta). Right: head of woman (Mathura).

love of exaggeration so dear to the Hindu character. Women are given extraordinarily large breasts and hips; gods with four arms are also something of a jolt for a European; but most of these figures are at least striking, which is more than can be said for the stiff, gloomy statues of our Middle Ages, or for most Egyptian works.

While ancient sculptures abound, paintings of comparable age are extremely rare, consisting mainly of the frescoes found in the 5th century underground temples at Ajanta. They lack perspective, but the figures are perfectly drawn and have a living quality about them. They are definitely preferable to the cold paintings of Byzantium; moreover, at the time they were painted, it would probably have been impossible to find a painter in Europe who could have done better.

Unfortunately, later paintings have been lost. A study of the miniatures in the ancient manuscripts, none of which dates from before the Moslem invasions, does not make it seem likely that the Hindus later improved a great deal on their predecessors. During the Moghul period, they formed part of the Persian school of painting.

Ever since the earliest times, metalwork has been the most widely practiced art in India. Although really ancient objects have become increasingly rare, doubtless because of the many wars and invasions which have taken place in India, some have been found which date from just before the birth of Christ. The regions bordering on Kabul,

that is, Kashmir and the Punjab, have always excelled in working gold and silver. But India on the whole has produced admirable work in gold, copper and bronze.

Since porcelain and china were not used at all in India for domestic purposes, the art of making objects out of bronze and copper reached a high level of development. Some of the bulbous vases, with thin, elongated necks, called *lotas,* which are used for carrying and storing water, are exquisite examples of the craftsman's art.

The art of inlaid metalwork, or damascene, and the art of covering metals partially or of inlaying them with opaque or transparent enamels has been practiced in India for many centuries, to a degree of perfection never attained by other peoples.

The peoples who invaded India, whether they came from Persia or from Europe, brought with them the arts with which they were familiar; as we have seen, these arts were promptly adopted and transformed by the Hindus. The art of inlaying precious stones (topaz, turquoise, jade, coral, amethyst, sapphire, agate, etc.) into white marble, which originated in Italy, was practiced for many years at Agra, where it reached extraordinarily high standards under the Moghul princes, who used this type of decoration for the walls of their palaces.

Another area in which Indian craftsmen have set standards with which the West can hardly compete is the manufacture of carpets, silks and shawls, etc.

As can be seen from fragments found in the

most ancient palaces in Iran, the use of enamelled bricks as a wall-covering on monuments, which was very widespread in northwest India after the Moslem invasions, is of Persian origin. Enamelled-brick facing is to be found on monuments in all parts of the Orient and must be counted among the most extraordinary architectural sights in the world; for example, the mosque of Omar, in Jerusalem, various monuments in Lahore, the palace at Gwalior, etc.

When seen from a distance, their multicolored façade, the transparent colors of which have a rainbow-like quality about them, gives the impression that one is looking at a fantastic palace built by some magician.

The Hindu arts, which were created by a race of poets with more of a gift for imagination and feeling than for reasoning, are capable of conjuring up before us an entrancing world of grandiose epics, of dazzling luxury and of wild fantasy.

Left: painting in temple no. 17 at Ajanta. Opposite: Dravidian statuette. Next page: top of a 16th-century pagoda at Ellora.